*Dr Lynn Parr is a w
wildlife, history and the rural landscape. She has
edited UK magazines including* Horse, The
Curlew, Artists & Illustrators, *and* This
England, *and her writing has appeared in
magazines such as* Horseman, Equestrian Life,
Western Horseman *and* Essex Countryside.
www.lynnparr.co.uk.

Books by Lynn Parr

Dangerous Secrets!
Still Waters: Fragments of Nature & Place
Cowgirl: A Home on the Wyoming Range
The History and Ecology of Hainault Forest
County Curiosities of England

CHAMPIONS OF THE HORSE

Saving Rare Breeds

LYNN PARR

Southwind Books

CHAMPIONS OF THE HORSE
Saving Rare Breeds

Second edition 2017

Copyright © Lynn Parr

All rights reserved
ISBN 978 0 9550 1842 8

First published in the UK by Southwind Books in 2012

Southwind Books
Caerwedros, Ceredigion, UK

Front cover: Friesian, courtesy of Janine Mason, Friesians Scotland
(www.friesiansscotland.com)
Back cover: Takhis, courtesy of Forestry Commission Wales

Contents

Introduction	7
A Valiant History	11
Dawn Horse to Desert Orchid	12
Mankind's Best Friend	18
What is a Breed?	30
Back from the Brink	35
The Caspian Horse	36
The Eriskay Pony	45
The Kerry Bog Pony	53
The Marwari Horse	59
The Friesian	68
Wild and Free	73
The Takhi	74
The Mustang	81
The Carneddau Pony	103
The Sorraia	112
Playing God	119
The Tarpan	120
Consequences	129
Handmade Horses	142
An Uncertain Future	149
On the Edge	150

Introduction

Riding the wind. Skimming the ground like an eagle in flight; leaving the world behind. Storm chaser; carrier of dreams. Who hasn't longed to be borne across the land by a fleet steed, breaking free of the bonds that tie us down? To many of us, the horse is nothing less than the physical embodiment of freedom. A dream; a desire made tangible. If only we could gallop away from all our fetters; be carried into paradise.

Throughout the long life of humankind, the horse has run alongside us, companion and friend, transport and slave. Even in the machine-bound West, when we now rarely need his services to plough fields or pull carts, we are reluctant to let go. We evoke a history that was never so gentle with our ploughing matches and parades of heavy horses. We ride now for pleasure instead of need.

But our relationship with the horse has always gone beyond mere use. He is much more than a tool – even if he has been abused as such by some. The horse is embroidered into our beliefs, our mythology, our religion – the Hodening Horse; the Nightmare; Poseidon's white horses of the sea; the Chinese symbol of courage and success; the Unicorn.

He has galloped across England's chalk downland for thousands of years. He prances and kicks in both ancient and modern Oriental artwork. His image decorates palaces from Middle Eastern prehistory, Native American tipis, Buddhist temples; cold caves across Europe. Even in our oldest stories, the horse plays a part. Not just accompanying human heroes in their adventures, but himself a hero, embodying the gods; blessed with magic powers, his name remembered down the ages – Bucephalus, the Godolphin Arabian, Red Rum.

He has carried us into war; enabled the conquering of settled peoples by nomadic tribes; helped us spread our species across the world in the first globalization – the Mongol hordes of Genghis and Kublai Khan, the Romans, the Normans, the Spanish Conquistadors.

And still he races and jumps for us, rounds up cattle, pulls coaches, masters complex manoeuvres in the dressage ring, carries us around the countryside – all for our entertainment. We sing about him, he stars in our movies, features in our literature.

Perhaps the Aztecs were right when they first saw the Conquistadors and believed man and horse were joined together: Perhaps we really are two halves of the same being.

○

Yet time and circumstance have not always been kind, and many breeds have disappeared. It is only through the efforts of some special people that we still have ancient breeds such as the Caspian and the Kerry Bog.

The people who have saved equine breeds from extinction have few things in common, apart from a deep love of horses. They haven't all been rich or influential; they haven't been experts in equine reproduction and taxonomy. In most cases, they haven't set out to become breeders and conservationists – they usually had something far different in mind as a career. Yet the one thing they do – or did – have in common is a drive that keeps them going; a tenacity that keeps them clinging on when fate knocks them back. Lack of money, political pressure, cultural obstacles – they have overcome them all for the sake of the horse.

What kind of people will try so hard to keep alive a dying breed? Why not let it go? Isn't that, after all, nature's plan?

Is it the collecting obsession, the drive that makes people spend all their waking hours trying to acquire a particular style of porcelain, a figurine from a movie series, a painting? Is it the idea of immortality: the laminating of their name so that it will last beyond them; a transference to another species that might last longer? Is it really similar to the passion felt by some people for the latest i-gadget, the obsession that replaces people with things?

No: I wouldn't go that far. Perhaps it is just the challenge and sense of achievement. Assuaging the guilt of mankind whose excesses have led to the extinction of so many species and breeds; the desire to put it right. A reluctance to let go of the past, to see a relic of a bygone age slip into the mists of history.

This book celebrates the efforts of just a few of the amazing people who have worked hard to save a breed of horse. The remarkable Louise Firouz, for example, who persisted in trying to save the ancient Royal Horse of Persia, despite being an American in Iran at a politically sensitive time – and who endured prison and the loss of her horses more than once, yet who just picked herself up and started again and again.

John Mulvihill has almost single-handedly brought a native Irish pony from his grandfather's stories back from the brink.

Then there is Francesca Kelly, who set a whole movement rolling in India, and enthused a new generation to appreciate the Marwari, an elegant link with their country's past grandeur.

The tenacious Velma Johnson, despite being disfigured by polio, took on the powerful US government in her campaign for humane treatment of the feral mustangs of the American West. Her efforts led to the current system of public land and wild horse management – along with the discovery of pockets of relict breeds that no one had thought still existed.

In Portugal, the accomplished scientist Ruy d'Andrade was responsible for preserving a remnant of the ancient Iberian Sorraia.

Others, too late to prevent extinction, sought to recreate a breed through selective breeding of similar types – for a cultural ideal in the case of the Heck brothers, supported by Hitler and Goering; or national pride for Polish university professor Tadeusz

Vetulani, all of whom attempted to bring back – or, rather, recreate – the Tarpan, Europe's first horse.

And then there's the amazing story of the Takhi, the strange Przewalski's Horse. Hunted to extinction in the wild but protected in zoos and private parks, it is now being released back on to the Asian steppe of its ancestors, a conservation success story that thrills the heart and gives you hope for the future of all wild and threatened creatures.

But what drives all these people? What special qualities make them so single-minded, dogged, forward-thinking? Whatever it is – shared with those who fight to save the tiger or an historical building – the world is richer for their persistence.

LYNN PARR

A Valiant History

Hay sled in Wyoming
© *Lynn Parr*

Dawn Horse to Desert Orchid

Unlike with most species, nearly everyone has heard of the horse's distant ancestor. There is, after all, something about the name 'the Dawn Horse' that touches the imagination. This little creature, whose skeleton was first found in the Tennessee Valley in 1867, has come to represent the very first equine, standing at the head of a long river of descendants getting bigger through the millennia until today's horse appears at the apex. It's a simple, romantic picture that we've been taught for more than a hundred years.

Our image of the linear evolution of Eohippus, the Dawn Horse, into Equus, the modern horse, dates from 1879, and was based on the extensive collection of horse fossils found by US palæontologist O.C. Marsh, from Yale's Peabody Museum of Natural History.

Marsh, along with British biologist Thomas Huxley, promoted the lineage as the perfect example of evolution in action, the horse arising as a North American forest browser and evolving into the grassland athlete of today. The picture seemed straightforward and elegant: a single line of species evolving from the distant past to the present. This model was perpetuated down the centuries, used to illustrate the principle of evolution for many species, and is still reproduced in books today.

Then, as with most of our long-held beliefs, science came along and spoiled everything. Now, although we still believe the horse evolved in North America, we know that the picture isn't that simple. Eohippus (now called Hyracotherium) is still thought to have been the ancestral equid, but the horse lineage was far from a straight line. In fact, we now know there were at least 33 equine genera – biologist Kathleen Hunt, of the University of Washington, says that Equus is 'merely one twig on a once-flourishing bush' of equids, but is the only genus that has survived.

Hyracotherium was a small, muntjac-like mammal living in North America's warm, wet forests around 55 million years ago (mya) during the Eocene period. The first horse had four toes on its front feet and three toes on the hind ones, with a pad like a dog's to enable it to cross the soft ground and marshes of its rainforest home. Instead of claws it had 'hoofies' on each toe. It probably looked more like a tapir – or even a dog – than a horse, standing around 25–36cm (10–14in) at the shoulder, with an arched back and possibly a 'camouflage' coat of light spots on a dark ground. It had teeth like a pig's that allowed it to browse on fruit and soft foliage like a deer.

Hyracotherium and its descendants altered very little in the ensuing 20 million years, except for changes in the teeth that allowed them to eat coarser foliage. Descendants included Orohippus, which gave rise to Epihippus, among others, which had five grinding cheek teeth.

As North America's climate began to dry out around 40 mya, wet forests gave way to grassland, and their mammals – including horses – began to change accordingly. Mesohippus looked more like a horse than a dog, its back less arched, its legs and snout longer. It also had three toes on both front and hind feet, with the fourth toe vestigial, though it still walked on the pads of its feet. It stood around 24in (60cm) high, had longer legs and snout than its forebears, and also had six grinding teeth for eating tough vegetation. Mesohippus also had a significantly larger brain. As with earlier forms, the genus Mesohippus consisted of several species.

But it wasn't the only horse in the paddock. Several Miohippus species split off from the Mesohippus line, and they all coexisted together, some in what is now Wyoming.

During the early Miocene period (24–20 mya), the Mesohippus

species had all died out, and the fossil record shows at least three new lines. One consisted of miniature horses, while another comprised the 'anchitheres', which moved into Asia and Europe across the Bering land bridge and remained as successful forest browsers for millions of years. The third line evolved into the horses we know today.

Around 20–18 mya, the North American rainforests gave way to treeless savannah and steppes with tough grasses, but many horse species adapted relatively quickly to these new conditions. Tall, high-crowned teeth evolved, which could grow continuously as the tops were worn down by abrasive grasses, and had a hard covering of cement. The neck became longer for grazing in a head-down position, and the position of the eyes changed to give all-round vision to watch for predators. Significantly, the legs became longer with springy ligaments and specialised bones and muscles for running, and the horse began walking on 'tiptoe' rather than on pads. Shirt-tail relatives at this time included Megahippus, which was the size of an elephant and covered in hair: but the genus that gave rise to today's horse was Merychippus.

So far, 19 species have been found in at least three groups during the 'merychippine radiation', an explosion of new species around 15 mya. Many species belonging to two of these groups, the hipparions and the protohippines, migrated to the Old World as plains grazers and forest browsers, the three-toed hipparions surviving until around 5 mya to leave their footprints among those of early humans found by Mary Leakey in East Africa. The other group led to the true equines.

It was Merychippus species in this last group that began to lose their vestigial side toes and stand on a single hoof, and they looked more like our own horse, built for grazing and running on the plains. Researchers testing a horse's running technique have concluded that it is now the most efficient running animal on earth.

Until recently, it was believed that one these species in the last group, Pliohippus, was the ancestor of Equus, but the discovery of Dinohippus seems to have scotched that idea – Dinohippus had straight teeth like the modern horse, whereas Pliohippus's teeth were definitely curved.

Eventually, one of the Dinohippus species gave rise to Equus, the genus of all modern horses. The Equus species (again, there were many) were about the size of a small pony, with high-crowned, crested, cement-covered teeth for grazing; a central toe with side ligaments that stabilised the hoof; long legs with fused bones that prevented rotation, and strong, springy ligaments under the fetlock. (The modern horse still retains the genes for side toes, which sometimes develop as splint bones each side of the hoof. Very occasionally, some horses are even born with fully formed toes.)

During the first ice ages, 2.6 mya, some Equus species crossed to Africa and evolved into zebras, while others moved into the Middle East and North Africa and became onagers and asses, adapted to desert living. Still others moved into South America, while some spread across Asia, Europe and the Middle East, becoming the true horse we know today.

Through DNA analysis of fossils, researchers now believe the first caballine horses (*Equus caballus*) appeared around 300,000 years ago, when there were numerous equine species and genera around the world.

However, by the last Ice Age, 10,000–11,000 years ago, only two species were still left in the horse's original home, North America. Researchers still can't agree on the exact cause of this extinction, which claimed many other large mammals, such as sabre-toothed cats and giant sloths, as well, but it's thought that a changing climate was partly to blame – and the fact that early humans had just reached the continent at this time is rather too much of a coincidence to be ignored.

All the horses soon became extinct in North America, and only a few Equus species survived in the rest of the world. These are with us today as zebras, onagers and wild asses, the domestic horse and the Takhi, or Przewalski's Horse.

After the ice retreated, the caballine horse evolved into two subspecies: the Tarpan, *Equus caballus gmelini*, the light, fast horse of the eastern European steppes; and the Forest Horse, *E. c. sylvaticus*, a heavier, stockier animal living in northern European marshlands, which became the heavy horse breeds. The Takhi (*E. ferus Przewalskii*) may or may not be a separate species – although it can hybridise with the domestic horse to produce offspring that can breed successfully.

These subspecies then evolved into four forms, two northern and two in the south: Pony Type 1 (Form I) was found mainly in northwest Europe. It was adaptable to harsh conditions and resistant to wet weather. It was generally brown, with a 'mealy' mouth and lighter colouring on flank and belly. Today it is represented by the Exmoor Pony, Britain's oldest breed. The other northern form was Pony Type 2 (Form II), which was bigger (14–14.2hh), heavier and coarser. It was found mostly in northern Eurasia, and could also withstand the cold. It was ancestor of many draught breeds, as well as the Highland Pony.

The two southern forms were horses, rather than ponies. Horse Type 3 (Form III) stood around 14.3hh. It had a long, narrow body, and long neck and ears. Found in Central Asia, it could tolerate a hot climate, and is represented today by the Sorraia, Andalusian and Barb. Horse Type 4 (Form IV) was smaller (12hh) and more refined. It had a concave profile and high-set tail. Found in the western Asian steppes and deserts, it was also heat-tolerant. It was the ancestor of the Arabian, and is represented by the Caspian.

Within these various forms are three groups (excluding the ponies); hot-blooded, cold-blooded and warm-blooded horses. The hotbloods are the fiery, fast Arabs and Akhal-Tekes; the coldbloods are represented by northern European breeds such as the Belgian; while the warmbloods had both hot- and cold-blooded ancestors. They are represented today by breeds such as the Trakehner.

So here we are today with a wide variety of horses, from the tiny Falabella to the giant Shire; the dainty Caspian to the muscular Welsh cob – all one species. As well as in green paddocks, horses live in the hottest deserts, on windblown steppes, in icebound Siberian valleys. Where they have escaped the bonds of domestication, horses gallop and fight and breed just as their ancestors did.

We may not have the diversity of equids that the world once saw, but who's to say that some isolated populations of feral horses won't eventually evolve into new species, given enough time and the right conditions? After all, it happened at least once, and though the little Dawn Horse isn't looking at us along a straight road of descendants as we first thought but through a tangled thicket, the changes from the first dog-like forest browsers to the most efficient running animal in the world have been incredible.

Who knows what the next few millennia will bring to what scientists call the most adaptable animal on earth?

Shetland Pony
© *Lynn Parr*

Mankind's Best Friend

Imagine riding a gazelle. Or hunting down, killing and butchering a horse for dinner. Neither of these images seems plausible today, yet to our ancestors, they must have been familiar concepts.

For long before the horse became part of mankind's domestic livestock, it was seen just as modern-day hunters see wild antelope and deer – as game ripe for the taking. And as for catching and riding an animal that ran wild like the gazelle… well, that was about as useful as making a hat for a bear.

Then someone thought out of the box. And once that idea had taken root, mankind suddenly wondered how he'd ever managed without the horse.

During the last Ice Age, around 10,000 years ago, herds of wild horses were still being driven off cliffs and clubbed to death. Large deposits of bones and cave paintings depicting hunting at places such as Lascaux, France, and Santander, Spain, show us how important the wild horse was to our hunter-gatherer ancestors as long ago as 35,000 BC. At Salutre in France, the bones of 10,000 horses were found at the base of cliffs, where they had been driven by Cro-Magnon man around 50,000 years ago.

The horse was hunted both for its meat and for its skin, and such was the demand that it's likely that the first humans to reach North America actually wiped out the continent's native horses just after the ice retreated, along with other large mammals such as the woolly mammoth.

The horse was the last animal to be domesticated by Mesolithic man, after the dog, sheep, cow, goat, chicken and pig. The dog was first, around 12,000 BC, raised from puppyhood as a companion and to help with hunting and warn of danger at night. Flocks of sheep were being tended by pastoralists by 9,000 BC, and the dog was then trained to help with herding.

Cattle were also kept on semi-open range around this time by people who had given up a completely nomadic hunting lifestyle and grew crops in the river valleys – particularly in the Fertile Crescent between the rivers Tigris and Euphrates in Mesopotamia (now present-day Iraq). Fowl were probably raised first for ritual sacrifices, then for eggs and meat.

People who remained nomadic on the Asian steppe were also probably used to herding hoofed mammals, much as the Sami in Lapland and the Mongolian nomads still do today. Indeed, it's thought that reindeer may have been the first semi-domestic hoofed animal, followed on their migrations from China across Outer Mongolia by nomadic tribes relying on them for meat, milk, hide, sinew and fat. Reindeer, which ranged much further south than they do today, were certainly herded and domesticated for about 2,000 years before the horse was tamed. In northern Europe, reindeer had been trained to pull sleds and carry riders by 5000 BC.

It was a natural progression, therefore, to try out herding skills on the herds of wild horses on the Asian steppe. Horses didn't have fixed migration routes tied into consumption of a particular food as reindeer looked for reindeer moss, so they could be directed to go where the herders wanted. They could also dig through snow to find vegetation and water more easily than reindeer, and were stockier and stronger for pulling. By around 4,000 years ago, early farmers were herding semi-wild horses and exploiting them for meat and milk.

But herding was only part of the story. Researchers have found evidence that horses were being ridden far earlier than first thought – and at least a thousand years before the invention of the wheel.

Until recently, a site at Dereivka, Ukraine, was thought to have some of the earliest evidence of horses being domesticated, around 4500–3500 BC, with the discovery of antler cheekpieces, possibly used with sinew or rope bridles. But a settlement of the Botai culture at Krasnyi-Yar on the Kazakhstan steppe has pushed back known horse domestication even further – possibly to around 5,500 BC.

In a settlement of 160 houses with adjacent fenced enclosures – possibly corrals – archaeologists have found numerous bones of young male horses (suggesting that they were culled), horse teeth showing wear from bits, bridle cheekpieces and roofing material containing horse dung. The site shows that steppe nomads had a good reason to settle down into a village: and that reason was probably the domesticated horse.

Early Iron Age graves found in 1929 in Pazyryk, in the Altai Mountains of Siberia, show that the horse was being put to good use around 3000 BC. In barrows in the permafrost, ancestors of the Scythians, one of the earliest known horse cultures, buried horses wearing reindeer masks complete with antlers; perhaps indicating that their owners herded reindeer on horseback, with the horses 'in disguise'.

Horse teeth worn by bits seem to confirm that the horses were, indeed, being ridden. Other well-preserved grave goods included a felt wall hanging of a man on horseback, and a saddle cloth decorated with human scalps.

Many of the riders buried with their horses were women, dressed in riding clothes with bows and other weapons. The bodies of riders and horses were all perfectly preserved, complete with skin, hair and tack – so well preserved, in fact, that it was possible to identify two types of horse.

One was short and stocky, resembling the Takhi of Mongolia – these were in some numbers in the graves. The other was taller, with longer legs and a more refined head, like the modern Turkaman, or Akhal-Teke. In all the 'kurgans', or barrows, there was only one of this thoroughbred-type horse, usually old or lame, whereas the many horses of the other type were killed at all ages to accompany their owners to the afterlife.

So who first tamed the horse? Was it people from Northern Europe, or is it just that the archaeological evidence is preserved well in certain regions while other sites have perished?

Recent research using DNA analysis has shown that a minimum of 77 mares from different populations spread over a wide geographical area would have been needed to account for the wide genetic diversity of horse breeds we know today. This means that probably hundreds of different geographic regions saw domestication of wild horses at different times.

The research was conducted on mitochondrial DNA – genetic material passed only down the maternal line. Since this material accumulates mutations at a known rate, it can act as a 'molecular clock', enabling researchers to trace a particular lineage back through time.

If ancient breeding practices were the same as today, in that only one or two stallions were used to cover many mares, then there could be much less genetic diversity shown in the lineages of the Y chromosome (the DNA carried down the paternal line). This would mean that far fewer stallions were originally domesticated and used for breeding. Research is ongoing.

And who devised the first bridle and bit? No one can know for sure whether the methods of horse domestication arose simultaneously around the globe, or whether there was a single method that was adopted via trade and other links between societies – although the widespread diversity of breeds and genetic traits suggests that it was the technology of capturing and taming wild horses that spread between societies, rather than the horses themselves.

Whoever domesticated the first horse, however, the idea quickly caught on, spreading across Europe into China and Arabia. And from then on, whoever had the horse had the world.

The first herds of semi-domestic horses were probably just mares, since stallions would have been too much trouble. When they were in season, the mares would probably have been staked out on the steppe to attract wild stallions for mating – a practice still followed today by people who own semi-domestic herds. Young males would have been gelded to reduce their natural aggression.

But breeding would have been very difficult unless the foals were brought up with the social interactions of a herd. Even in relatively modern times this was evident, in the many failed attempts to breed the Mongolian wild horse, the Takhi.

In the open steppes, riding and herding may have come about at roughly the same time, since it would have been easier to keep a herd of horses together – or to lead it – from horseback. However, in some cultures, wheeled vehicles appear in the historical record before saddlery, hinting that horses were driven before being ridden, particularly in regions such as Asia Minor, where the horses were small, and it was considered undignified to ride them.

For example, in Sumerian graves in the Tigris-Euphrates valley, solid wheels have been found dating from 3500 BC, while in Mesopotamia onagers (a type of wild ass), controlled by nose rings, were used to pull chariots before the Hyksos, nomadic tribes from Asia, introduced the horse around 1700 BC. Similarly, horses in bronze bits and harnesses appear in Egyptian bas-reliefs dating from around 1360 BC.

By 3000 BC, entire cultures revolved around the horse, particularly in the steppelands. The horse provided all their needs – meat, milk, hides for clothing and footwear, dung for fuel, bones and hooves for tools and musical instruments, currency and transport. And since nomadic people needed ever more grazing land for their herds, as well as staples such as salt, the next step in the domestication of the horse was logical: trade or war.

Some of the first people to use the horse in combat were the Elamites and Kassites from present-day northeastern Iran. Around 3000 BC they conquered lands to their west in what was to become Persia. But the most efficient early empire based on the horse as an instrument of war was that of the Hittites.

During the second millennium BC, Hittite warriors invaded the region now called Anatolia in Turkey; no one is sure where they originated. Then they gradually spread across Asia Minor until they controlled most of Syria, as well. Babylon (in present-day Iraq) fell in 1595 BC, and the Egyptian Pharaoh Rameses I found to his cost that the Hittites were a powerful enemy – the Battle of Kadesh, Syria, in 1286 was the biggest chariot battle of ancient times, with the Hittites fielding more than 17,000 infantry and almost 4,000 chariots.

And it was the horse-drawn chariot that was the main reason for Hittite superiority on the battlefield. It's not known exactly when the chariot first appeared, but the first models had solid wheels. The Mesopotamians had spoked wheels by 2500 BC, and the war chariot was being used across Europe, Asia and China by the turn of the millennium.

It was the Chinese who invented the breast-strap harness, which was much more efficient – and kinder to the horses – than the original system of throat and girth harness and wooden yoke, which had been used for draught oxen and onagers.

Later, an even bigger breakthrough was the trace around the shoulders. This increased efficiency and power so much that a single horse (probably a cross between the Tarpan of Europe and the Mongolian wild horse) was able to pull a cart carrying six people. Historians think the Chinese were able to easily invent such a system for the horse because of their tradition of people pulling boats up canals using a similar harness.

Like many, the Hittite war chariot carried a driver, shield-bearer and an archer or javelin-thrower. Two horses were hitched to a central shaft, each with another horse to its outside. The harness had been adapted from the yoke used by oxen, and the horses were controlled with bits across their lower jaws.

A Hittite horsemaster, Kikkuli, wrote a celebrated horse training and husbandry manual around 1350 BC, in which horsemen were advised to feed their horses chaffed straw, lucerne and grain. Written in cuneiform on clay tablets, it was one of the first instruction manuals to link equine nutrition with exercise to build condition and stamina, and was also the first instruction in interval training, detailing a seven-month programme to build up a horse's stamina and strength.

Kikkuli's programme was tested in 1991 at the University of New England, Australia, and was found to be a very effective method, bringing a horse up to a high level of fitness while keeping it sound. Kikkuli trained the Hittite cavalry to become superb horsemen, no doubt contributing greatly to the superiority of King Suppililiuma's forces in battle.

Many other empires were built following the Hittites' example. The Celts spread across Europe, the Hyksos invaded Egypt and the Aryans conquered Persia and India. The Assyrian chariot, seen in reliefs in the North West Palace of Nimrud dating from the 9th century BC, was driven by one standing man while an archer fired alongside him. The horses were strong and muscular, with decorated manes and tails. A century later, mounted warriors were riding stallions into battle alongside chariots.

On a lighter note, the horse also brought another innovation to the Western world from the Asian steppes – trousers. Before anyone in the Mediterranean region rode horses, they wore togas or tunics, but once the horse was established, the Romans and Celts adopted tight trousers, or leggings, for their cavalry.

By 600 BC, the Persian empire was the most powerful in the East, using the Nisean horse, which may have been a cross between the Tarpan and a small, fine-boned breed of Horse Type IV.

It may also have been an early Caspian Horse, though it was much bigger than that later breed, appearing in carved reliefs to be around 15hh or bigger.

Persian riders used padded saddlecloths but no stirrups; archers steered with their knees as they fired their arrows. The Assyrians and the Babylonians also used the Nisean horse.

For the Persians, the horse was a status symbol, and only the aristocracy were allowed to own one. As well as being employed in battle, horses were raced over courses of 11 km (7 miles) and used for hunting and in an early form of polo.

The Persian chariot had two shafts extending from the sides, and the horses were controlled by a long yoke across their backs. During the summer, Persian horses roamed pastures in the foothills of northwest Iran.

Horses were also used in tribute – a Medean province once paid a Persian king in pasture for 50,000 horses, while the

Armenians gave tribute of 20,000 foals a year. By contrast, the Cilicians paid one white horse for every day of the year.

In the Persian empire, the horse was even used in the first postal system, a kind of Pony Express. Stations were one day's ride apart, and the riders rode without stirrups.

Running an empire was a constant struggle with usurpers, and the nomadic horsemen from the East were ever-present threats, particularly the ferocious Scythian tribes from the south Russian steppes, one clan of which was the Parthians. The Parthians were excellent horsemen and archers; they developed the 'Parthian shot', an archer firing an arrow over his horse's tail at full gallop.

The Parthians and other Scythian tribes united around 800 BC and embarked on a series of wars, eventually gaining a foothold in Persia once the Persians were defeated by Alexander the Great. They occupied the northern part of Persia for almost 40 years. Like most horse-owning cultures, their wealth was measured in horses, and they gave us the first records of gelding young colts.

Horse-drawn chariots were also used by the Ancient Greek and Roman empires. Indeed, one of the earliest accounts of horses being used in Greek battle is in Homer's *The Iliad*, written around 800 BC, in which warriors used chariots pulled by two horses, but dismounted to fight on the ground.

Greek horses were too small to be ridden at that time; though 400 years later, a larger horse had been bred that could carry warriors into battle where the terrain was too difficult for chariots.

Horses were imported from the East and bred with Greek horses from Thessaly for Arab-type refinement, and also with larger Persian and Scythian horses to produce larger, stronger horses for riding. As in other cultures, the horse was a status symbol, with only the upper classes being allowed to own one.

The Greek General Xenophon (c 430–356 BC) wrote a respected manual for training cavalry. *The Cavalry Commander* describes how mounted soldiers could scout in advance of the army and then the cavalry would ride across the enemy's infantry, throwing javelins. Chariots at the rear of the army would be loaded with spare javelins.

Both the Greeks and Romans were fond of chariot-racing – it was even an Olympic sport in 680 BC, when chariots were pulled by four horses, like those in the movie *Ben Hur*.

Two-horse chariots were being raced by 408 BC, and though riders also raced on horseback, it was not as prestigious as chariot-racing. The Ancient Greeks also fought bulls on horseback. As well as chariot racing, the Romans bred horses for the circus, parades and hunting.

In the Middle Ages, horses took the Moors sweeping across Europe in the 8th century AD – and helped Frankish knights defeat them at the Battle of Poitiers in 732.

The Moors rode small, wiry horses (around 14hh) with short stirrups, standing up in the saddle to bring all their weight down behind their swords. The Franks, on the other hand, rode large, heavy horses – perhaps Percherons or Friesians – standing around 15hh. The riders sat back with their legs braced in front – the first time stirrups had been used by Europeans – and formed a wall of steel with their armour.

This technique had been perfected by Charles Martel, the Hammer of Christendom, when he had reorganized heavy cavalry in Gaul to fight the Moors in 711. This wall effectively blocked the Moorish attack, and then, when the knights charged, the Moorish riders were scattered.

Martel's grandson, Charlemagne, continued to use heavy cavalry, and eventually drove the Moors from northern Spain.

In the Americas, the once-indigenous horse was reintroduced by the Spanish Conquistadors and became an essential part of life for the plains tribes, such as the Apache, Navajo, Cheyenne, Comanche, Sioux and Nez Percé.

Originally, most horses were acquired by trading or theft, rather than breeding, but the Nez Percé in Idaho soon developed the Appaloosa (also called the Palouse or Tiger Horse), while the Chickasaw, among others, bred Colonial Spanish horses.

On the plains, the horse transformed the lives of its owners, turning them from a pedestrian group who lived in forests and by agricultural fields into a buffalo-hunting, nomadic culture.

It was a huge status symbol and used for tributes and as currency. It was painted for war and ritual. It was killed and buried with its deceased owner so it could be ridden in the spirit world. The bravest warriors took its name for their own: Crazy Horse, Black Horse, Little Horse, Red Horse, Sorrel Horse, Spotted Tail, White Horse, Old-Man-Afraid-of-His-Horses.

Imagine the Wild West without the horse: No Indian wars, no cavalry and Custer, no cowboys, no Pony Express, no stagecoaches. Perhaps covered wagons would all have been drawn by oxen, as many were – but how could Jesse James or Butch Cassidy have chased down a train (an 'Iron Horse') on an ox or escaped from a bank robbery on a bicycle?

Even today, ranches in Wyoming, Montana and Colorado rely on horses to move cattle between ranges, while hunters take pack strings of horses into the mountains every autumn. Here, the horse is still king of its rugged terrain.

China, which had its own small, indigenous horses, imported finer breeds, such as the Akhal-Teke, from Ferghana (now in Uzbekistan). These fine horses also provided the foundation stock for many European and Asian breeds, including the first 'Arabians'. As in other cultures, the horse was a symbol of wealth and status in China, as well as a bringer of success.

In Europe, William of Normandy took 3,000 horses on 700 ships to England in 1066, and his cavalry gave him the upper hand against the English at the Battle of Hastings, who also rode into battle but then dismounted and fought on foot.

In the Middle Ages, large warhorses, known as 'destriers', were bred especially for mounted combat and war games such as jousting, their size and power giving extra force to the impact of a knight's lance (rather than simply for bearing the weight of a knight in heavy armour, as popularly supposed).

Sometimes nails were left sticking out of their shoes so that they could trample enemy infantry. It was expensive to own a horse, so only the landed gentry could afford one. However, because of the feudal system of land tenure, in which peasants were allowed to farm strips of land in return for working on the lord of the manor's land, ordinary people had access to horses for agriculture.

As well as the heavier breeds favoured for war, lighter, fine-boned horses were bred for riding by the gentry; Oliver Cromwell imported Arabians for use in cavalry during the English Civil War. Horses were also indispensable during the numerous wars between England and France.

In 1701, Jethro Tull invented the horse-drawn seed drill, heralding a new era in agriculture and even more reliance on the horse. In the county of Kent alone, there were 23,000 farm horses in 1898.

No one seeing the parades of Shires and Suffolks in the fields, the Cleveland Bays hauling stagecoaches and the Hackneys pulling carriages in the cities could have doubted that the horse ruled the world.

And no one would have believed it could all change so drastically.

However, by the end of the 19th century, horsepower was all but obsolete, replaced by steam. The last of the village and farm horses were rounded up at the beginning of the 20th century and taken off to the First World War.

Then the internal combustion engine was invented, and although some horses were kept for leisure riding and racing was popular, thousands were destroyed, many draught breeds dwindling almost to extinction.

In many countries the horse is still used to pull carts and ploughs, skid logs from forests and round up livestock, though in most places it is now largely a pet, rather than a vital piece of equipment.

But from the first wild horses captured for meat to Alexander's Bucephalus who helped conquer half of Europe; from El Cid's Babieca, who drove the Moors from Spain, to Comanche, who stood loyally beside his fallen rider on the battlefield of the Little Bighorn even while Custer's Seventh Cavalry lay dead all around him; from the Greeks' winged Pegasus to the Celtic goddess Epona galloping in chalk across the Berkshire Downs, to racing legend Desert Orchid: there is nothing else on earth quite like the special relationship between the human and the horse.

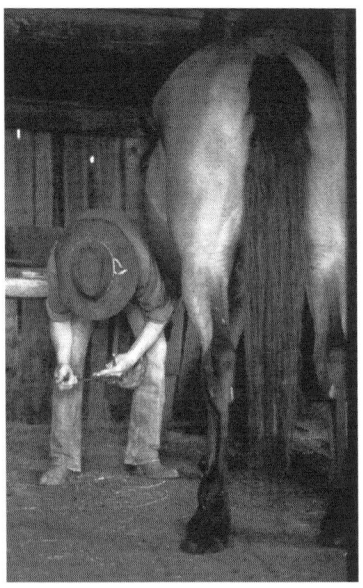

American Saddlebred
© *Lynn Parr*

What is a Breed?

No one knows just how many breeds of horse are in the world today. We recognize certain types, of course, classified by the four main shapes.

From Arabians to Shires, Falabellas to Thoroughbreds, all domestic horses belong to the same species, and while they may not find mating – or pregnancy – very easy, they can all, theoretically, mate with each other.

So exactly what is a breed? Put simply, a breed is a population of animals with similar characteristics that distinguish them from others of their species, and whose breeding is restricted so that those traits are consistently passed on to their offspring.

In some respects, a breed is an artificial term applying only to domestic animals that have been selectively bred by humans. It is the breeders (or breed societies) who determine the breed standard, and it's by the common consent of other breeders that only animals registered as meeting that standard are mated with others with the same traits, thus reproducing the characteristics of that type in a predictable way.

A breed can thus be created or conserved artificially – for example, in horse breeds with a closed studbook, which will only register foals whose parents and ancestors are known and registered.

Breed societies may also introduce their own restrictions into the studbook by only allowing registry of horses of a certain colour, such as the black Friesian, thus selecting for an even narrower set of genetic traits.

The American Cream Draft breed was created from a single mix-blooded draught mare, 'Old Granny', who was put up for sale in Iowa in 1911. She was mated to other heavy horses with the same colouring – cream coat, pink skin, white mane and tail and amber eyes – from Percherons to Belgians, and her offspring that fit the preferred profile were mated with similar horses.

By 1944, there were enough cream-coloured horses of this type, with a registry recording all matings and foalings, that a breed society was formed, and four years later, the State of Iowa Department of Agriculture recognized the American Cream Horse as a standard breed.

By contrast, some studbooks are 'open', accepting registry of similar, but specified, types. In the US, for example, this means that Appaloosas can be outcrossed with Arabians, Thoroughbreds or Quarter Horses, while Quarter Horses are allowed resulting from matings with Thoroughbreds.

However, because only specific, similar, breeds are allowed into the mix, and a certain variability in inheritance is allowed, the genetic base of each breed is still conserved (most of the above stem from a common ancestor).

A breed can also develop its distinct traits through being geographically isolated so that individuals will have only mated with similar ones for thousands of years – the Icelandic Horse, for instance.

Likewise, the Exmoor Pony, the oldest equine breed in the UK, has remained the same for thousands of years. Attempts at cross-breeding failed when the hybrid offspring were unable to survive the harsh conditions of Exmoor.

According to equine genetics expert Professor D. Phillip Sponenberg of the Virginia-Maryland Regional College of Veterinary Medicine, although each breed may have some diversity within it, it is generally uniform and produces offspring that are predictable. This consistency has arisen due to selective breeding over a long period of time.

Each breed has a "unique combination of genetic traits". This is why conservation of all breeds is important, he adds: it is directly conserving the genetic diversity of the entire species – the horse's genome is all contained within the domestic breeds, since there are no more truly wild horses (the Takhi is not an ancestor of the domestic horse).

Without wide genetic diversity, a species may lose some of its adaptability and may be more vulnerable to diseases or disorders that can threaten a particular genetic type.

Unfortunately, fashion dictates which breeds are perpetuated – some are always going to be more popular than others. Modern breeding has "converged on a very few popular international types," says Prof. Sponenberg, with most breeds gradually being fitted into these pigeonholes, either by outcrossing or selection.

The problem with this is that some ancient, less-popular, breeds, such as draught horses, may eventually be lost forever, simply because their looks have gone out of fashion.

In recent years, genetic analysis has enabled researchers to look back into the past of many equine breeds and determine how they got where they are today – and, more importantly, where they are going.

The latter point is particularly important because so many populations disappeared at the end of the 19th century once the horse ceased to be used for transport, agricultural work and general riding, while genetic 'bottlenecks' caused by inbreeding in small populations leads to disorders and extinction.

Once a breed carrying its own unique gene pool becomes extinct, there is no way to recreate it, and inherited attributes are lost forever, preventing future breeders from incorporating those traits into new breeds and improving current ones.

The first genetic research on the horse investigated the Takhi, or Przewalski's Horse, in 1995, establishing that it was not an ancestor of the domestic horse, but actually sat on a side 'branch' of the horse family tree.

Studying the mitochondrial DNA (mtDNA – genetic material passed directly down the female line without recombination), the Japanese researchers also concluded that the change in the number of chromosomes (the Takhi has 66, compared to the domestic horse's 64) occurred relatively recently.

Since then, several studies have been conducted on various bits of the horse's DNA, even comparing it to genetic material found in the remains of ancient horses. The conclusion from almost all the studies is that there are so many variations within each breed, it is impossible to determine the breeds' origins.

However, there is a greater 'genetic distance' between northern European and Asian breeds and those originating in the south, represented by the Thoroughbred.

The trouble with using mtDNA as a genetic blueprint is that it does not show the effects of the male side of the equation, so the overall picture can only be guessed at, particularly with the time-honoured method of breeding many mares to only one stallion – though this is why mares are considered to have contributed more diversity to the horse genome than stallions. Studies on the Y-chromosome, passed down the male line, may give more answers.

It doesn't always take eons to produce animals that differ physically from others of their species in another environment. For example, the feral horses in the Namib desert have adapted to their hostile environment over only a century. They are around 10cm shorter than their ancestors and grow a thick coat in winter to protect themselves against the bitter cold of the desert nights.

Their grazing and drinking behaviour are different to those of other horses, too. Living on the sparse, tough, poor-quality vegetation of the Namib, when conditions are good they will graze for 17 hours of 24, compared with other semi-wild herds, such as the Camargues in the wetlands of France, which graze for 13 hours each day.

They can also go without water for much longer than usual – between 30 and 72 hours, though some have been known to last 100 hours. In this respect, they are more like other native desert species, such as the oryx, than domestic horses.

Although it's unlikely that there have been genetic adaptations in such a short time, the horses are so inbred that they already have a different genetic makeup to any other breed, and they have an unusual component to their blood whose function is, as yet, unknown. Dr Gus Cothran of the University of Kentucky, who has bloodtyped the Namib horses, believes the unidentified component may eventually prove to be a crucial adaptation to their harsh environment.

These remarkable desert-living horses are just one example of how the species can adapt to life in the most inhospitable terrain, in a wide range of conditions.

At the other extreme, the Yakut horses of Siberia live a semi-wild life in temperatures of −65°F (−18.3°C), their thick coats protecting them from the snow and wind.

Different appearances, adaptations, behaviour; different breeds: yet all the same species. From lush green pastures to hot deserts to windblown steppes, the horse has conquered the world. Who's to say that the environmental adaptations of the Namib and Yakut horses will not prove crucial to the existence of the entire species in centuries to come, particularly with the drastic changes forecast due to global warming?

Wild mustang in Nevada
(courtesy of US Burea of Land Management)

Back from the Brink

Marwari dancing at HM The Queen's Diamond Jubilee Pageant, 2012
(courtesy of Royal Windsor Horse Show)

The Caspian Horse

Refined heads tossing disdainfully, high-set tails flying out behind, the small, fine-boned horses pull the chariot of King Darius the Great of Persia into a lion hunt without hesitation or fear.

These dainty, exquisite horses depicted on the great seal of Darius in the British Museum are not the ideal equids of an artist's imagination: this was a real breed, known not only to Darius in 550 BC, but to the Egyptians a thousand years earlier – perhaps even to Mesolithic hunters, who drew its likeness on their Asian cave walls.

This was the Royal Horse of Persia; an ancestor of the Arabian and other light horse breeds – the original Horse Type 4.

While it is thrilling to see what this breed looked like in ancient images, what is even more astonishing is that we can see it today in the flesh. For it still exists, in what is almost certainly the same form – making it the oldest domesticated breed of horse in the world.

But it was very nearly lost altogether, and its road to recovery was rocky. It is now called the Caspian Horse, and its survival from extinction is due to one remarkable woman.

Once you start to look, you find the little horse described in ancient writings and depicted on artefacts from across

Mesopotamia and Asia Minor – for instance on a terracotta plaque from the Second Millennium BC, now in the British Museum, which depicts a Caspian being ridden with a nose ring.

An archaeological dig at Hamadan, Iran, found 10,000 bones, including those of a Caspian-type horse. In earlier ancient Mesopotamian digs, equine bones were believed to be those of the onager, a type of wild ass, but modern DNA analysis is challenging those theories.

Bas-reliefs on the walls of Darius the Great's palace in his capital, Persepolis, dating from c 522-486 BC, show that the little Caspian played a prominent role in Persian royal ceremonies, being considered precious enough to be presented to visiting kings as gifts.

Small and swift, able to manoeuvre at high speed in a confined space, it was also used to pull chariots in arenas, where Persian kings killed lions to demonstrate their fitness to rule.

In the reliefs, Caspians attend the investiture of King Ardashir in AD 224, while King Shapur is shown riding a small horse in AD 260, his feet almost touching the ground.

Caspians also pull a similar gold chariot dating from the 4th or 5th centuries BC in the Oxus Treasure, the most important collection of silver and gold from the Achaemenid period of Iran, discovered in the late 19th century and now in the British Museum.

After the Moslem conquest of Persia in AD 627, however, the horse disappears from historical records.

Modern DNA tests have established that the Caspian is genetically a miniature horse, not a pony, and has unique haemoglobin, the protein that transports oxygen in the bloodstream.

A slim but muscular neck supports an Arabian-looking head with a dished face, almond-shaped eyes, large nostrils and small ears that sometimes curve inwards. The tail is high-set. The colour of the fine, silky coat is mostly bay or chestnut, with the occasional black or grey, and sometimes a dorsal stripe, showing the breed's wild ancestry. In winter, a dense coat is grown, enabling the Caspian to tolerate harsh weather.

Extensive research has revealed that the Caspian has distinct skeletal differences from other breeds. Studies in 1969 found that the skull is slightly different, with a unique formation of the parietal bones (forming the sides and top of the skull), which show a pronounced elevation, known as a vaulted forehead, though there is no parietal crest.

There is an extra molar in the upper jaw where wolf teeth may appear in other breeds – the Caspian is said to be more of a browser than a grazer. The shoulder blade, or scapula, is wider than other breeds', and the leg bones are longer and slimmer in relation to height, which allows for more speed, despite the small stature of the horse – it is said to be able to keep up with other breeds in all gaits except gallop.

The first six vertebrae are longer than usual, giving the appearance of high withers and a straight back. The length of the legs, narrow back and strong hindquarters produce a long, free-flowing gait. Due to its mountain origin, the Caspian has more angled hocks than lowland breeds.

It stands 10–12hh, but some modern-bred individuals have only been 9hh, which is thought to be closer to the ancestral size. The foot has an extremely hard, narrow, oval hoof – more like an ass's than a horse's – which rarely needs shoeing. The frog is not as pronounced as that of other horses. Despite its fine appearance, the Caspian's bones are very dense and sound, and it can traverse rocky ground easily, is agile, and has a natural ability for jumping.

Louise Laylin, from Great Falls, Virginia, was mad about horses. Living on the family farm, where her parents bred horses, she rode to school each day. She wanted to be a vet, but unfortunately, physics proved a stumbling block, and that dream floated out of reach.

Louise switched to Classics and English Literature, but during her Junior year at Cornell University, things took a dramatic turn that was to lead to a life far different to anything she could have imagined, and entangle her in events that would reverberate down through the years.

Spending the year at the American University of Beirut, Lebanon, Louise met Narcy Firouz, an Iranian aristocrat related to the previous Iranian royal dynasty, the Kadjars. When she finished her degree in 1957, she married him and moved to Iran.

After six years in Shiraz, Louise and Narcy established the Norouzabad Equestrian Centre in Tehran in order to teach children how to ride.

"Our children were learning to ride and their friends wanted to join them," she told me. But there were only hot-blooded local stallions available, which were totally unsuitable as mounts for children.

On earlier trips around the country, Louise had noticed small, even-tempered horses living near the Caspian Sea. So in 1965, she set out with two other American women and an Iranian to look for suitable horses for their children to ride.

"The local villagers were suspicious but very friendly and hospitable," Louise recalled. "We didn't know exactly where to look for the horses. It was just luck that we started in one of the better places."

In Amol, in the remote Elborz Mountains in the north of the country, the women found a small stallion pulling a heavy cart. The stallion, to be called Ostad, was covered in sores and lice, as were two other similar horses, the stallion named Aseman and the mare Alamara. They saw another 30 small horses running almost wild along the shores of the Caspian Sea, between Amol, Babol and Kiakola in the Elborz Mountains, while a further 20 with similar characteristics were found across a wide area.

To her amazement, Louise realised they were identical to the horses depicted in the reliefs at Persepolis.

Excited by her discovery, Louise had seven mares and six stallions bloodtyped, and their bones and DNA tested. The tests established that the horses were, indeed, of the ancient breed, ancestor of all hot-blooded horses. Instead of being extinct, the royal horse of Persia was alive, if not entirely well.

Once she'd discovered that the native horse was still to be found, at least in remote areas of the country, setting up a breeding programme seemed the logical thing for Louise to do.

"I didn't set out to breed the Caspian," she said with a laugh. "It was curiosity more than anything else, and I had no idea it would go as far as it did."

The breeding programme took off with gusto. In 1970, the Shah of Iran helped set up the Royal Horse Society, with Crown Prince Mohammed Reza Pahlavi as its patron, in order to preserve the country's native breeds. The society bought Louise's foundation herd of Caspians, relieving her financial burden, but allowed her to continue running the stud in Norouzabad until 1974, when it took over operations itself.

Britain's HRH Prince Phillip and Princess Anne (now the Princess Royal) visited the Shah for the 2000-year celebrations in 1972, and attended a ceremony at the ancient palace of Persepolis. They also visited the royal stables and watched children as young as five racing Caspian stallions.

Prince Phillip was concerned that there were so few of the ancient breed, and that they were all in the same region. He offered to take care of any that could be exported to the UK. The Shah presented him with the stallion Rostam and the mare Khorshid Kola, and these established the European foundation herd.

The horses were held in quarantine for two years before being allowed to enter Britain, during which they produced a filly, named Atesheh. Two mares and a stallion were also exported to Bermuda.

Between 1971 and 1976, a total of nine stallions and 17 mares were exported to England and Bermuda.

"The Royal Horse Society helped by allowing us to ship the horses – or some of them – on Imperial Iranian Hercules airplanes," Louise said.

Of the Caspians exported to Europe, some were eventually sent to set up herds in Australia and New Zealand. By now, Louise had another herd of her own, in northern Iran, consisting of 20 mares and three stallions.

But then everything started to go wrong. Suddenly, being an American in Iran was like being an American in Afghanistan today, and all Louise's hard work was destroyed. Indeed, it was touch and go whether she would even survive the crisis herself.

There had been discontent in the country for several years, with widespread protests about the unequal distribution of wealth from oil sales, and a perceived 'Westernisation' of the Iranian culture.

The Shah, who had succeeded to the throne upon the death of his father, Reza Khan, in 1941, had been involved in a power struggle with his prime minister, Mohammed Mossadegh, over nationalisation of the country's oil industry. The US believed that Mossadegh was trying to ally Iran with the Soviet Union, so the CIA masterminded an operation to oust him.

In return for guaranteeing the US a steady supply of oil, the Shah received military and economic aid. However, he cracked down hard on those who opposed his policies, refusing political freedom. In 1963 he put down an uprising led by the nationalist Islamic clergy, and sent its leader, Ayatollah Ruhollah Khomeini, into exile.

In the next decade, the Shah spent billions of dollars on weapons, fuelling support for the dissenters. In 1977, in a crackdown on exports of national assets, the Royal Horse Society banned further exports of Caspians, and Louise's horses were seized by the Imperial Government to form a national stud. She was only allowed to keep one, the stallion Zeeland. But this was not the end of her troubles.

By January 1979, the political climate had deteriorated beyond repair, and the Shah was forced to flee to Egypt. The Ayatollah Khomeini returned to lead the nationalists and whip up anger against the US and Americans living in Iran.

Louise and Narcy were arrested and imprisoned.

"I was one of many, and the reasons were probably multiple," she remembered. "I think being an American during the American hostage crisis would have been sufficient."

In November of that year, protesting about the Shah going the US for cancer treatment, students overran the US Embassy in Tehran and took more than 70 Americans hostage. They demanded that the Shah be returned to Iran to face charges and that billions of dollars he had 'stolen' from the country be returned. Some hostages were released after subsequent negotiations, but 53 remained captive in the embassy for an entire year.

Fortunately for Louise, her ordeals as a captive did not last that long. On one occasion, she resorted to drastic measures to be released: hunger strike.

"It seemed like a good idea at the time," she reflects. "And I suspect it got me out faster, as my husband, Narcy, ate everything and he stayed in for three months, while I only stayed in two weeks."

During the 1980-88 Iran-Iraq War, the national herd of Caspians was lost when the horses were sold off to nomadic tribes as pack animals or for meat. Famine and upheaval made it very difficult to feed the horses, so Louise grazed them in the wild.

Then she lost two of her best mares and a foal to wolves, so organised an emergency evacuation of seven mares and a stallion to the UK. As punishment, the Royal Horse Society seized her remaining Caspians.

"They were herded into a field near Gonbad and eventually either died or were sold off to Kazakhs, who eat horsemeat," she said.

Louise also had "a bit of other trouble" during the war, but didn't want to elaborate to me, as "it's already gotten me into further trouble since then for mentioning it."

After the war, however, Louise was allowed to develop two more breeding centres with Caspians captured from the wild or bought – one centre set up for a German businessman and one for a Canadian.

In 1994, Louise found some more feral Caspians and a few in a large stable, none of which was related to the European herd. In defiance of the government – and at great personal risk – she exported seven of them to the Caspian Stud UK via Russia and Belarus, where they survived attacks by bandits.

That same year, Narcy died. Louise was forced to sell her herd to the Ministry of Jehad through financial necessity, due to estate settlement and the expense of exporting the horses to the UK.

By 2007, things had calmed down a bit since the dangerous days of the Islamic Revolution and Iran-Iraq war, but in the volatile international climate, Louise was aware that she could not afford to become complacent.

She switched her efforts to breeding the Turkaman, or Akhal-Teke, another ancient Iranian breed, which may have been the original 'Arabian' that eventually resulted in the Thoroughbred.

In 1999, with help from supporters in Canada and the US, she was able to start up a breeding programme for Turkaman horses with two stallions and eight mares. She soon had 45 Turkaman horses on her farm in Gara Tepe Sheikh on the steppes, on the border with Turkmenistan.

"I didn't really rediscover the Turkaman," she told me. "That was a known item but neglected, and people around the world were ignorant of its past. The research on the Caspian naturally included other forms of core Oriental horses."

She was not sure about whether her farm would ever again be home to the little horse she spent so many years saving.

"I don't know about breeding the Caspian anymore, but we are certainly highly involved in the Turkaman," she said. "I'm still really busy, what with 45 horses, guiding foreign trekking riders and answering emails." With sponsorship, she occasionally attended conferences around the world to speak about the Caspian.

And as for the Caspian itself? Although the local people are very supportive of her efforts, Louise said things are still not perfect for the little horse in its native land.

"It is difficult in Iran, where breeding and exporting are not encouraged. But those that get out have a fine future."

There are still only a few hundred Caspians around the world, and only a handful of breeders, but at least the breed looks secure, thanks to Louise. But, typically, she was modest about the part she played in its recovery.

"Many times I considered giving it all up, but there were always too many dogs and horses to seize that opportunity."

But despite her ups and downs and the current climate of mistrust between cultures, Louise was fatalistic about her life. When I asked her whether she still had problems with the government, her reply was understated but telling:

"Nothing new."

Louise died in 2008 at the age of 74.

Caspians
(courtesy of Caspian Horse Society)

The Eriskay Pony

Two things you may think you know about the Outer Hebrides: Whisky galore! and Bonnie Prince Charlie. What you may not know is that both are associated with the little island of Eriskay.

And, like most people, even in Scotland, you are probably unaware of the tiny island's third claim to fame – a little pony that may have been known by the mysterious Picts 2,000 years ago.

On July 23, 1745, a French ship drew near to a windswept beach on the island of Eriskay: and a legend began. The ship brought Charles Edward Louis Philip Casimir Stuart – 25 and nicknamed Bonnie Prince Charlie for his good looks and inspirational leadership.

He'd come to claim the thrones of Scotland and England from the Hanoverian George II. His father was James Edward Stuart, the Old Pretender, whose half-hearted attempt to restore his Catholic family to the throne occupied by George I – grandly called "the Fifteen" for the beginning of the uprising in 1715 – had ended in humiliating failure.

But by the time the Young Pretender arrived in Scotland, old mistakes had been swept under the rug and his Jacobite followers were ready to try again. [The nickname 'Jacobite' arose from the Latin for James, *Jacobus*].

Unlike his father, the son of James II, the prince was dashing and accomplished – he played golf and the violin, loved dancing and was an expert archer with the crossbow. He was also charming, and though he couldn't speak much English, let alone fluent Gaelic, he learned a few phrases in Gaelic and some Highland airs, which he would whistle to keep up the morale of his men and endear him to his people.

Although he had arrived with only seven men, Charles brought a ship full of weapons, and once word had spread, more than 700 Cameron clansmen rallied to his standard on the banks of Loch Shiel, Glenfinnan, on August 19. By the time the army was ready to march on London, it had swelled to more than 5,000.

The Highlanders first marched to Edinburgh, where Charles was proclaimed king of Scotland and England. And when the Highlanders defeated General Sir John Cope's 3,000 English soldiers at Prestonpans in September, the cause seemed destined to be won.

Storming across the border, avoiding the forces of General George Wade in Newcastle, the Scots took Carlisle on November 14, Preston on November 27, Manchester two days later and then Derby on December 4. Now they had only 127 miles to go to London.

The capital was in a panic. Wealthy people fled with their jewels and silver, and there was a run on the Bank of England. The king even had the royal yacht made ready for a quick getaway to the continent. No one could quite believe this was actually happening.

But then, to the Jacobites' dismay, everything started to unravel. Charles had counted on French reinforcements; but it soon became clear that, just like in the Fifteen rising, they weren't coming.

And neither were the hordes of Jacobites supposedly ready to join him in England. Worse, the king's son, the Duke of Cumberland, had been recalled from Flanders, and now waited in Staffordshire with 8,000 redcoats.

The Highlanders began to lose heart. To advance would be to get further away from reinforcements; further from any hope of escape should things go wrong. Even the prince's advisers recommended retreat, with the promise of regrouping in Scotland with Scots and Irish troops sent by France, and another attempt on London the following year.

Reluctantly, the Jacobites crossed back into Scotland in December, with the English army in hot pursuit.

But even though the winter saw more supporters gathered to the cause, particularly with small victories against English outposts, the death knell was about to be sounded for the rebellion. The Highlanders were running out of money and arms, as well as food, while the English were continually receiving food and supplies from boats landing every day on the coast.

Then, in April 1746, desperate from frustration, and despite advice to the contrary, Charles made a decision that would seal his fate – and reverberate down the centuries. He decided to attack Cumberland's army on Culloden Moor.

But there were 3,000 redcoats more than wearers of the tartan. And this time, having learned from the Highland charge that had defeated General Wade, Cumberland's troops used a new tactic: instead of attacking the Highlander directly in front (who was carrying a shield), each soldier bayoneted the enemy to the right, catching the Scots on their unprotected sides.

Consequently, more than 1,200 Highlanders were killed this way, while the English lost only 76 men. Afterwards, Cumberland earned himself the nickname 'the Butcher' from ordering that the wounded Highlanders on the battlefield be bayoneted to death.

After this crushing defeat, the rebellion broke apart. The Highlanders fled back to the west coast, where they took fishing boats for France. The prince managed to get to South Uist in the Outer Hebrides, only just evading capture when local lady Flora Macdonald dressed him up as her maid.

For five months Charles and a handful of supporters wandered the Highlands, travelling on foot, by boat and on horseback, sleeping in barns and caves and in the open, helped by sympathizers, only one step ahead of the English army.

But even though the redcoats stole crofters' cattle, broke their ploughs, burned their houses, raped their women and caused the death of hundreds through famine and exposure to the elements, no one gave up Bonnie Prince Charlie to them, even with a price of £30,000 on his head.

Eventually, after saying goodbye to Flora Macdonald on the Isle of Skye – inspiring The Skye Boat Song – the prince managed to find a boat to take him back to France. He lived on for another 42 years and died in Rome in 1788, a drunken, broken man.

In Scotland, his story grew into a legend, particularly when the Duke of Cumberland took out his frustration at the prince's escape by punishing the clans. No one was allowed to wear tartan; the chiefs' hereditary posts were abolished; the ownership or wearing of a sword or other weapon was forbidden. Anyone suspected of being a Jacobite was evicted and executed.

Twenty years later, the old clan system was dead. But the romance of Bonnie Prince Charlie lives on today in songs, monuments and a parade of Highlanders in Derby on the anniversary of the day that England nearly had another Stuart king instead of a German.

And though it seems an age ago, old wounds take a long time to heal: in London's Hampton Court Palace is a portrait of the Butcher of Culloden – but it is considered too inflammatory, even today, to be put on display.

On Eriskay, a stone cairn marks where Charles first stepped ashore, and a rare pink flower is said to have sprung up where he dropped its seeds from his pockets.

It was the middle of the Second World War. Rationing was in full swing; people had grown used to doing without. But on the Hebridean islands of Barra and Eriskay, a far worse crisis was looming than merely making do with powdered eggs: the supplies of whisky had run out.

But the Lord works in mysterious ways. By coincidence, the SS Politician left Liverpool on February 4, 1941, loaded with 25,000 bottles of whisky bound for the USA. Somehow, the crew became disoriented and thought they were further south – and the islanders couldn't believe their luck when the ship ran aground off Eriskay in the middle of the night.

The crew were taken off in boats, but then began weeks of

wrangling between the authorities about whether the cargo of 'The Polly', as it was known colloquially, could be classified as salvage.

But some on the island had already made up their own minds, and the cases of whisky began disappearing.

Customs chief Charles McColl made it his personal duty to stop the pilfering and recover all the missing cases. He and his men raided every house on the island, confiscated boats, patrolled the sea around the ship night and day, and arrested 35 men and a 14-year-old boy. Some men were accused simply for having oil on their clothes – there was oil spilled in the hold of the ship.

Eventually, McColl saw 20 men go to prison in Inverness for stretches of 20 days to three months. But even after all that, most of the whisky was never recovered.

And the story would have remained a local legend, if it hadn't been for the novelist Compton Mackensie, who lived on nearby Barra. He turned the story into the novel *Whisky Galore!* in 1948 – *guleoir* being the Gaelic for plenty – and it was made into the classic Ealing film in 1949.

The local pub is now named after the ship, and keeps a bottle – ruined by salt water beyond drinking now – behind the bar.

The Outer Hebrides are not for the faint-hearted – or the lazy. The climate is harsh, the landscape unforgiving. Everyone has to pay his way. In earlier centuries, particularly, survival meant fishing and crofting – self-sufficiency by growing what few crops would thrive in the wind and salt spray, and raising chickens and pigs. The Western Isles could only be reached by boat, so once you were there, you generally stayed.

Part of this landscape of toil and hardship was a little grey pony only about 12hh. Its tough, waterproof coat enabled it to live out in the harshest weather, and it could scramble across the roughest terrain without losing its footing. While the men of the households were out at sea, the pony helped the women and children by hauling panniers of seaweed to strew on the fields as fertilizer, or turf to burn on the fires.

Known as the 'Back-door Pony', it also pulled little carts or harrows when called upon, carried children on its back, or dragged a light plough. Like the Kerry Bog Pony across the Irish Sea, only docile and willing individuals were kept; aggression or stubbornness were selected out by culling.

But island life was changing. On islands closer to the mainland larger horses, such as Clydesdales and Norwegian Fjords, were being bred with the native pony to produce an animal that was taller and stronger. From this strain would develop the modern Highland Pony. But because of their remoteness, Eriskay and Uist retained the last few pure-blooded native ponies. By 1968, only 20 remained on Eriskay.

Then biologist and crofters' commissioner Alasdair Fraser visited Eriskay. He saw the little ponies and realised that they had an unusual and distinctive appearance. When he mentioned this to vet Robert Beck, formerly of the Edinburgh (Royal Dick) Veterinary School, who had retired to Tiree, he discovered that Dr Beck was also interested in the ponies. So the two decided to try and find out more about the breed.

"They discovered only a few, the last of the Western Isles ponies, indigenous to each island," says Mary McGillivray of the Eriskay Pony Society and an Eriskay breeder for more than 20 years. "They felt that it would be such a pity if they did die out."

The two got together with Father Callum McNeill, the priest on Eriskay, who was known and respected by the entire community, and Dr Robert Hill, a GP on nearby Barra, who knew of some breeding ponies owned by crofters.

Other people who became interested in saving this old breed included Dr Richard Allen, a zoologist from Edinburgh, and Eoghann McLachlainn, a local crofter on South Uist. Together they formed a breed society and named the little pony the Eriskay.

At first, no one could find any purebred stallions left, so the group decided that the best course of action was to take the finer type of Highland Pony (developed from the original Western Isles Pony in the 19th century) and breed back with pure Eriskays to recreate the breed. But then one pure stallion was found.

"Someone had bought him and hadn't realised there was all this panic going on," says Mary. The stallion was named Eric; he went on to have three sons.

The Rare Breeds Survival Trust became interested in the group's efforts and oversaw bloodtyping that established that the Eriskay was a distinct breed.

No one knows how the Eriskay got to the Outer Hebrides, but it must have been there a long time – Robert Beck noticed that many Pictish marker stones on the islands and on the mainland had carvings of small ponies, and from measuring their proportions, he concluded that the animals could well be Eriskays.

The Western Isles Pony was probably a descendant of the ancient Northern European breed that also gave rise to the Icelandic, the Exmoor and the Shetland.

The Eriskay Pony could have been drawn up out of the landscape itself, fashioned from stone and sand and wind. Born black or dark bay, upon reaching maturity the coat invariably changes to grey – like the lichen-speckled rocks that edge the shore.

The thick tail is low-set so the pony can wrap it around its rump for warmth. Its coat is dense and waterproof; its hooves hard. There are fine feathers or tufts on the fetlocks. Bred for manual labour, its shoulders are sloping, and its long ribcage and short loin make for a strong back. The overall impression is that the pony is square.

With its inbred hardiness, the Eriskay can also live out all winter without a rug, unless it is clipped for work.

"They are much happier outside," says Mary McGillivray. "Their coats are very thick. But if they live in a paddock system different to their native heath, they do need shelter. Even a heath has trees and rocks; a bare paddock is much harsher than a heath."

Like the olden days when they could survive by eating seaweed, the ponies are easy to look after, Mary adds. "They are very tough and need little feeding. If they've got extensive grazing and a lot of coarse herbage, their natural diet, they need very little hay." Mary's own ponies only receive concentrated feed if they are working.

But it is the temperament that most endears the Eriskay to owners. "They have a gentle nature; they're very people-oriented," says Mary. "We do tell people who take them on that they love people so much, they can be a bit pushy. Children like competing on them and we do encourage people to do different things."

Owners now use Eriskays for carriage driving, dressage and show jumping. "They are very athletic and quite fast for their size," Mary says. "They've great stamina, so that is a help. They are steady and don't get in a flap if they get stuck somewhere."

But though there are Eriskays from the Isle of Wight to the Orkneys, only a few have so far been allowed to be exported. "We don't really want to split up the very small breed at the moment," Mary says. "The gene pool is too small to send some off to some far-flung place."

Although there are now between 400 and 500 individuals, the status of the Eriskay Pony is still classified by the Rare Breeds Survival Trust as 'Critical'.

"There are so many people whose enthusiasm has got the Eriskay where it is today, but the breed is definitely not saved yet," says Mary. "People have got to see the work with the ponies and will say 'Oh gosh, they're absolutely wonderful ponies'. Something that really endears itself to you."

So if you are at an agricultural show and see what looks like a square grey, nondescript pony, don't dismiss it out of hand. Just take a minute to recall its small, windswept home, and remember that you are looking at a direct link with centuries of history, heartache and triumph.

Eriskay Pony
(courtesy of The Eriskay Pony Society)

The Kerry Bog Pony

In the Fifties and Sixties, the West of Ireland was rural and remote. Most people lived off the land, subsisting on fishing and a little farming. Their fields were fertilized with seaweed; their homes were heated with open fires fuelled by peat, or 'turf'.

And since there was no motorized transport, everyone walked or drove a trap pulled by a small native pony. It was a jack-of-all-trades, and almost every family had one. It had been this way for centuries; people expected it to be this way forever.

Known as a "hobby", the shaggy, sturdy little pony had been in Ireland as long as anyone could remember. It was used for hauling the family to Mass, carrying the children to school, and carting the turf bricks cut from the peat bog to the drying place.

In this latter job, the pony would cross the bog to the peat diggings dragging two poles of holly or birch behind it like a Native American travois, to which was fixed a huge, double-woven reed basket. When the basket was full of peat bricks, the pony would drag this "turf slide" to the road, and two men would catch up the basket and turn it over to unload the turf. The pony also carried panniers of seaweed from the rocky shore to the fields to be used as fertiliser.

But the old ways were gradually dying out. Many ponies were transported to France during the Napoleonic Wars to be used by the British Cavalry as pack animals or for meat. Hundreds of small farmers and crofters died or emigrated during the Famine in 1845, and those who remained turned to the donkey, which had been imported from Spain in the early 19th century.

Farmers wanted taller, stronger horses to work the new machinery on larger, consolidated farms. The hardy little native ponies were left to fend for themselves on the peat bogs and marginal land.

John Mulvihill of Glenbeigh, County Kerry, had heard stories of the little ponies working on the bog from his grandfather, Conn. His father, Jeremiah, ran a turf yard in Limerick in the 1950s and '60s, and before switching to a V8 Bedford lorry, he used the little ponies to deliver the turf around the city.

"When he returned to Listowell, he spoke of the pony, which he called the 'hobby', or the old breed," John says.

"He had a pony called Patrick, about 10.2hh, who was never shod. When they went out on slippery roads he put flour sacks on his hooves, and off they went, delivering turf, bringing in seaweed, or to the creamery."

John had also read an old book about Kerry – "and lo and behold, there were the ponies. The author described huge herds of little shaggy ponies. And it dawned on me; is it true, I wonder, is there a special breed of Kerry pony?

"The book said how you could give the ponies their head and they would descend the deepest crevices and climb the steepest hills. I wondered if any had survived in the hills of Kerry.

"But I was really only interested in big horses – I kept a couple of registered Irish Draught mares and a Connemara mare, and bred Thoroughbreds, and I never had any interest in ponies. I thought small ponies were worth nothing."

John owns The Red Fox Inn in Glenbeigh, and one night the chef's car broke down and John gave him a lift home after work.

"We stopped for a little while in Glencar and had a little sip of whiskey. And I looked out of the window and there was a little chestnut pony, no bigger than a Shetland. I said to the owner, 'I see you've got a little Shetland there'. And he said it wasn't a Shetland, it was one of the old breed."

John was smitten with the little stallion, which was only 11hh and had a flaxen mane and tail, and decided there and then that he had to have him. Luckily, he managed to persuade the owner to sell him.

Now that he knew that the native ponies still existed, he became determined to breed some and set about trying to find more. But there was only one problem: there were only about 20 of the ponies left.

John began publicising what he was doing, in an effort to get people to find the ponies and preserve what he sees as part of the country's heritage. Eventually, he found another stallion and a few mares, and bred his first foal in 1989. He called the breed the Kerry Bog Pony.

In 1994, upon hearing John interviewed on a radio show, Dr John Flynn of Weatherby's Ireland DNA Laboratories contacted him to ask where his research was leading. He suggested that John have his ponies bloodtyped. The results confirmed what John had suspected all along.

"We have found that, like most other breeds, there are different frequencies of genes present in the Kerry Bog Pony when compared with other breeds," Dr Flynn says. "The Kerry Bog has been selected out based on a number of criteria – for example, size and geographical location." In other words, the little pony that everyone used to see working on the bogs is a distinct breed.

John was delighted. The Irish Rare Breeds Directory registered the Kerry Bog Pony as "Ireland's heritage pony", and the Mulvihills set up a breed society to encourage and monitor breeding. Many of the ponies were named with their peatland heritage in mind: The Badger Queen, Bog Oak, Bog Cotton, Purple Heather and Old Peat.

"In the 17th, 18th and 19th centuries the bogs were huge, quaking swamps," John says. "It was only when people moved in with mechanical diggers to drain them that they shrank and dried out like today.

"If you look at pre-Famine times, so many people had good, strong horses; they had milking goats, a cow, ducks and geese, and little ponies tied up in the evening or hobbled and left on the old bohereen (road). The amount of grass they had was too valuable to let the ponies graze it – they were only contributing their labour to the family's upkeep. I have no doubt about it, looking back, that the ponies were probably cast aside as worth nothing.

"But I honestly think that we're living in a world of such waste. If people can't see a use for something, they throw it away."

The Kerry Bog Pony is usually around 10–12hh, in a solid colour such as chestnut, black or bay, often with white markings. and a flaxen mane and tail. The head is like that of a small Arab, with a dished face.

"The head is very neat, with little ears," John says, "not the heavy jaw and stumpy gait of a Shetland or Welsh pony."

Its teeth are hard and strong to graze the tough grasses on the bog. The pony's nostrils are large in proportion to its face, and it has a large heart and lungs to draw in plenty of oxygen to help maintain stamina. The coat is dense to withstand extreme conditions of wind and rain, and there may be some feathering on the legs. In summer, the coat is fine and silky. Its legs are strong and muscular, its cannon bone is short and flat, and its upright hooves are extremely hard to cope with the soft ground of the bogs. Unsoundness is very rare.

"It has a lovely, flat, solid hoof, and when pulling heavy loads, it spreads its hind legs so that each foot stands on a separate piece of ground," John says. "They are very powerful and strong, and very willing. If you let them have their head and don't force them, let them find their way, they'll do a bit of snorting but go down in the muckiest conditions, picking their way.

"The local vet, Teddy Clifford, said to me, 'I'd like to have them weighed and know what their strength is'. I had Flashy Fox on one end of a quin (the wooden part of a plough with a hook at each end), then Michael Clifford, who had several donkeys and was always so proud of them, brought up some donkeys.

"He hooked up a big black Spanish ass and there was a tug of war, but Flashy Fox held him. In fact, he held three donkeys! When the donkeys realised they couldn't pull, they just gave up and stopped. But the pony got down on his knees to pull."

Like the Eriskay, the Kerry Bog was originally bred as a family pony, so it has an excellent temperament. It is gentle, confident and well-mannered. Many are trained for carrying children or pulling small carriages – one even worked for the Riding for the Disabled. It can turn its hoof to anything.

"What the camel is to the Sahara, the Kerry Bog is to the bogs of Ireland," says John.

"There are two ends of the market we're aiming for: getting young children learning to ride – the Kerry Bog is easier than a Connemara, which is quite a big pony. And the other thing is driving."

To this end, the Kerry Bog is taken to shows all over Ireland and has even begun competing in its own class.

In 2003, a small breeding herd was exported to the US, though there are still fewer than 300 in the whole of Ireland, and many people have still never heard of the breed.

"We want to build up a good strong national herd before exporting too many more, " says John. He has now issued the first of the Kerry Bog Pony passports, and promotes the breed in the Kerry Bog Village, a museum of old buildings and crafts, in Glenbeigh. In 2005, the Kerry Bog Pony Society received a grant of €135,000 from the European Equisave programme to preserve rare equine breeds with close ties to the culture and history of Atlantic regions.

Even better, in September 2006, a genetic study was published that showed quite clearly that the Kerry Bog Pony comes from a different genetic line to other Irish breeds.

Dr Emmeline Hill, of the Animal Genomics Laboratory in Dublin, says the study of mitochondrial DNA (mtDNA – genetic material passed down the maternal line) "does suggest a certain isolation from other breeds. It has the highest proportion of the rare mtDNA type E in all global horse populations. This type E is found principally among pony populations of western Europe."

However, she adds, "although mtDNA data give us an insight into female maternal history, other genetic systems are required for a more informative perspective."

Nevertheless, "the Kerry Bog Pony population does harbour a rare genotype different from other Irish breeds. This has important implications for conservation."

Recent research has shown that the Kerry Bog is more closely related to Northern European breeds such as the Shetland and Icelandic ponies than to the Connemara, which roams Western Ireland.

John Mulvihill is delighted that researchers and other people are taking an interest in the breed that means so much to him.

"It's taken over my life," he says. "My wife says, if you'd put half as much effort into doing something else, you could have been a good businessman. The pony is the absolute love of my life."

Kerry Bog Pony
© *Lynn Parr*

The Marwari Horse

There's something different about the Marwari Horse. Strong neck and rangy legs, compact, upright body – you notice these things second. First, you notice its ears.

Like curved, razor-edged scimitars, the tips of the ears practically meet in the middle and always seem to be listening. Unlike most other breeds, its looks reflect its pedigree in a way you can't ignore: the Marwari looks perpetually poised on the brink of a cavalry charge.

And that, indeed, is its ancestry; as a noble charger carrying the royal princes of Rajasthan into battle. This was its saving grace: but also nearly its downfall.

The precise ancestry of the breed was lost centuries ago, but legend claims the first Marwaris were created in the feudal Middle Ages from an indigenous Indian horse bred with Arabians and horses owned by Alexander the Great. Its present conformation suggests that it does, indeed, have hotblooded ancestry, probably from desert breeds such as the Akhal-Teke of Turkmenistan, along with breeds indigenous to Kazakhstan and Uzbekistan, as well as the Arab.

By the 13th century, the Marwari had been developed into a showy, courageous battle mount by the ruling dynasty of northwest India. The kingdom of Marwar, in Maru Pradesh, the 'region of death', had been founded by the Rathores, a clan of the warrior caste called the Rajputs ('sons of princes'), who built hillforts, palaces and grand mansions in the deserts and mountains of the inhospitable northwest. Beginning with only around 200 horses, so traditional tales relate, after 11 generations the Rathores had conquered most of what is now Rajasthan and had a cavalry of 50,000 Marwari.

The Rajputs believed they were descended from the sun and moon, and had strict codes of honour and chivalry, claiming to be able to cleanse themselves of impurities with fire rituals. Over nearly 400 years, they fiercely resisted attempts by the Moslem Mughals to take over Rajasthan, even though the rest of India gradually came under Mughal control.

Eventually, the Mughal ruler Akbar, who came to power in India 1556, tried a new tactic to assimilate the Rajputs; he married the Rajput princess Rani Jodha Bai, and a new alliance was formed that was to last until the 17th century.

The Rathores had bred the Marwari Horse in their own image: proud, passionate, courageous. It could withstand extremes of temperature and cover long distances over rugged terrain with speed and stamina using its special pacing gait, the "revaal".

It was also trained to perform high leaps and kicks, once used in battle and now used to great effect in circuses and festivals.

Like other desert breeds, such as the Caspian, the Marwari Horse seldom needs shoes on its hard, oblong feet and is able to walk in sand and across rock, while its long legs and compact shape keep the amount of body surface exposed to heat radiating from the ground to a minimum.

It stands around 14.2–15.2hh; its silky coat – whose pattern of hair whorls is seen by local owners as inauspicious or foretelling good luck – coming in a range of colours from chestnut to grey, palomino to coloured.

The Marwari has exceptional hearing, allowing it to warn its rider of impending danger, while its strong sense of direction has resulted in many tales of Marwaris saving the life of a rider lost in the desert.

The Rathores regarded the Marwari Horse as divine and therefore superior to all other breeds, and even to people who were not of their caste. Apart from themselves, only members of the warrior caste, the Kshatriyas, were allowed to ride or even own a Marwari. They commissioned their bards to compose grand tales of heroism and glory in battle, not just of themselves, but also of their horses.

Today we might think that taking a horse into battle is hardly a gesture of love and respect for the animal, but for the Rathores, their horses were as much a symbol of their rank and their belief that the only honourable way for a warrior – and his horse – to die was on the battlefield.

Marwaris whose legends have come down to us today include the celebrated Chetak, a white stallion who carried Maharana Pratap into the battle of Haldighati against the Mughals. Chetak reared and drummed on the head of the enemy commander's war elephant with his forefeet, causing the elephant to panic, which allowed Pratap to kill the Mughal commander and resulted in disarray in the enemy's ranks. The Mughals were almost defeated in the ensuing mêlée, until their reinforcements arrived.

During the second Mughal advance, Chetak was mortally wounded when one of his hind legs was hacked off above the hoof, but he carried his master to safety over a mountain stream before dying in his arms. Chetak's name lives on in racehorses and children's games, as well as in a range of motor scooters.

Another famous Marwari belonged to the Rajput Amar Singh, who was chastised by a Mughal minister in the court at Agra Fort, but who cut off the minister's head and attacked the emperor Shah Jahan (builder of the Taj Mahal). Cornered on the battlements by the emperor's guards, he leaped his Marwari over the wall to drop 70 feet from the sandstone ramparts.

The horse was killed, but Singh escaped to his mansion before being captured. The Amar Singh Gate at Agra Fort and a statue of the horse commemorate this event.

The Mughal empire began to decline in the late 17th century with challenges by other kingdoms such as the Marathas – and as Mughal power began to wane, so did that of the Rajputs. The Marathas plundered Rajput homelands and extorted protection money – even from fiercely independent regions such as the Marwar, whose royal family in Jodhpur had never submitted to Mughal rule.

The Rajputs turned to the British for help and signed treaties enabling them to continue in positions of power. Their wealth grew with access to international trade, and they were able to furnish their palaces with jewels and carpets, silks and murals – including depictions of British bobbies, cars and hunting parties.

But their new alliance came at a price. When British rule ended in 1947, the Rajputs lost their power base. Even after the 22 states of Rajputana were amalgamated into the state of Rajasthan in 1949, the princes remained symbols of the hated British Raj.

In 1956, the new independent socialist government broke up the feudal kingdoms, stripping the Rajput princes of their titles, lands and possessions. And because the Rajputs had forbidden anyone not in the correct caste to own or ride a Marwari Horse, the Marwari, too, was regarded as part of the hated feudal system. Thousands of the Rajputs' prized horses were slaughtered, castrated or given to local farmers to be used as draught animals.

By the 1980s, tourism had become the biggest industry in India, with a lot of foreign interest centred on Rajasthan, where former maharajas and other landowners were capitalising on ancient traditions and festivals. Horse breeding was once again a major pastime in the region. Led by Maharana Bhagwat Singh of Mewar, who founded The Chetak Trust, other breeders established The Chetak Horse Society of India, whose main objective was to prevent the Marwari from becoming extinct and to raise its profile around the world.

In 1992, in an effort to conserve the gene pool and prevent further cross-breeding, the government included the Marwari and other indigenous horses on a list of national treasures whose exportation was illegal. It was only just in time: in the few decades since independence, the noble breed that had once numbered thousands and carried princes into battle had been reduced to only around 500 individuals.

Francesca Kelly encountered the Marwari Horse while on a riding holiday – and her life was transformed. Brought up in Egypt as the stepdaughter of the British Ambassador to Cairo in the

1960s, she had fond memories of desert life and galloping on desert horses under starry skies. So when she first saw Marwaris at a horse fair in Rajasthan, she fell in love.

"I grew up in the Middle East and have an affinity for desert horses because of what I grew up with," she says.

"Desert horses have an undomesticated aliveness about them, like a hawk – its vigilance and presence and awareness is incredible. The Marwari has the same alertness and vigilance. Most Western horses are half-asleep. They're horizontal, underworked, overweight. But the Marwari is a hundred per cent present.

"They're so exotic-looking. The Marwari has beautiful eyes, their ears are charming and unique, they're intelligent and receptive and very good-natured. The mares are like cats, they're so affectionate. And they're also elegant and very powerful and exciting to ride. It's like getting out of a comfortable saloon car into a racecar."

She decided to make the conservation of the Marwari the focus of her life, and bought six of them. But because of the export ban, she was not allowed to take them home. There was nothing for it: she would have to either sell them or breed them in India. Setting up a partnership with Raghuvendra Singh Dundlod, known affectionately as 'Bonnie', who had organized her riding safari, she chose the latter.

Along with other breeders they set up the Indigenous Horse Society of India (IHSI) in 1999 to encourage the breeding of high-quality Marwaris and raise awareness of the breed around the world.

But because it was a breed new to the majority of people, there was no consensus among breeders on how to even describe the Marwari, let alone produce a breed standard. Everyone had different ideas, and many other societies sprang up, in competition with each other rather than working together. It didn't seem likely that a proper breeding system and national studbook would ever be established.

There was also resistance to a foreign woman taking charge of breeding an indigenous Indian horse, in partnership with someone from outside Marwar.

So Francesca and Bonnie established their own breed standard, concentrating only on horses whose ancestry was known, since it would have been impossible to trace the Marwari's history back through the centuries like other breeds to find a foundation sire.

By 2000 she had won the 100km endurance race at the national equestrian games, and convinced the Equestrian Federation of India to sanction the first national show for indigenous horses.

By taking Marwaris to demonstrations and festivals all over India, she managed to boost interest in the ancient breed and encourage breeding. She and Bonnie also managed to get the government to accept the IHSI as the main Marwari breed registry, so that anyone wanting to compete or export the Marwari (the export ban was reversed in 2000) had to register through the society. Many veterinary organisations, including the National Research Centre on Equines have since accepted the breed standards of the IHSI.

"They're wonderful people to spend time with, but they're too competitive to link their common interests," she says. "So we have to go through the tedious process of government.

"There's still a lot of competition between breed societies, but the IHSI is accepted at government level. Ultimately, everything has to be accepted through governmental processes; important things have to happen through the government. It's quite amusing, really. We actually have the Maharajah of Jodhpur as a patron of the IHS, yet his people are in opposition to the society. He's in an unenviable role."

One of the ways Francesca boosted interest in the Marwari was to offer her stallion, Dilraj, for sale for $50,000 – a small sum by the standards of other pedigreed horses, but a fortune to local Indian horse traders – and breeders suddenly realised what a top-quality Marwari could be worth. Prices soared from a few hundred to several thousand dollars, and Francesca says breeders were given a powerful incentive to look after their horses and document their bloodlines. She didn't sell Dilraj then – he was destined to become famous.

However, even after the export ban was reversed, Francesca's first shipment of Marwaris to the US, where she lived with her American husband, was not straightforward. European Union laws prohibited the horses from landing anywhere in Europe, in case they brought contagious diseases. Then, upon reaching the US, one of her mares tested positive for piroplasmosis, a tick-borne disease found in many indigenous Asian horses. The mare was not allowed to pass through Customs, and Francesca spent 10 weeks – and $15,000 – trying to persuade authorities not to euthanise the mare. Eventually, a vet arranged for the horse to be treated in Venezuela, which cost another few thousand dollars but at least allowed Francesca to keep the mare.

Once in the US, with the horses safely at her stables on Chappaquiddick Island, Massachusetts, Francesca set about promoting the Marwari across the country. She attended exhibitions and shows, got advertising agencies to use the Marwari in photographs, gave demonstrations of 'tent-pegging' – spearing a four-inch wooden block at the gallop. But it was hard work.

"The US doesn't have the same connection with India as Europe," she says. "We get an enormous number of requests [to buy Marwaris] coming through, but I will not separate horses. If three or four can go to start a small herd, that's fine. But a lot of people just want a horse to put in their backyard. I love the breeding, but ultimately something had to happen."

And then, something did.

In September 2006, Francesca's stallion Dilraj became the first Marwari to enter Europe when he joined the Musée de Vivant Cheval (Living Horse Museum) in Chantilly, France.

"They created a show around the Silk Route, an Asian-influenced spectacular of theatre and dance," Francesca says. "They renovated the entire site without government subsidies. The father wanted to breed the Marwari. But they'll have to be very aware of the situation in India: France is not high on the Indian breeders' agenda, as the French eat horseflesh.

"I couldn't've come up with anything better. We are both dedicated in our own way and in different ways. They really wanted to explore India, and I arrived at the right time. We told them that they could only safely import Marwaris through the IHSI, and they have an express wish to breed."

Pascal Renauldon, husband of Sophie Bienaimé, who manages the Musée de Cheval, says it was very important for the family to have Dilraj.

"He was the first Marwari horse ever to be imported into France, and also an important piece of my wife's show, 'On The Silk Road'. For this show, we were in Mongolia, China (where we bought some costumes) and India (where we bought some tack) and where we met the Marwari Horses. After our travel, we were then thinking how to integrate a Marwari into the show, and then Francesca made her proposal. It is great and so generous."

As everyone expected, Dilraj was a huge hit. "It was a real success for the Marwari Horse," M. Renauldon says. "Every visitor took a photos of him and we had 3TV here specially for him."

Francesca had no doubts about Dilraj being a success in France. "He learns incredibly quickly," she says. "He loves to work – he's a little star. Dilraj is so beautiful, he needs to be seen; he needs to be shown." He has now become the "standing stallion" for Spain.

Dilraj made a fleeting visit to the UK in 2012 when he danced with seven other Marwaris at HM The Queen's Diamond Jubilee Pageant at the Royal Windsor Horse Show. The horses' visit was sponsored by Francesca and her partner, rather than the Indian government, due to the difficulties still being encountered over export of Marwari horses.

"We are right now fully immersed in pushing IHSI and a national petition for fair export policies, currently and in past years hampered by the opposing Johdpur Marwari Horse Society who have blockaded export, insisted on branding the horses registered with them (which 90% of indigenous stakeholders oppose) and using their connections through the Johdpur Palace to confuse the government. For instance, no one wants to brand their horses and the Indian people know that they cannot sell a branded horse to an Indian consumer. However, the MHS Johdpur have decreed that unless the horse is registered with them, branded as proof of registration and supports their policies, any other Marwari is not a Marwari, merely a half-breed. This, of course, does not go down well with the rest of the country."

While Dilraj sets about taking Europe by storm, Francesca continues to breed the Marwari Horse in the US and at Dundlod

Fort in India. After all these years, she knows what she is looking for when seeking out high-quality Marwaris to buy.

"If you know a breed, whether a Spanish or a Shetland, you know which characteristics to look for. I know most of the good horses in Rajasthan and the Punjab. I'm familiar with where they come from and the bloodlines. I know what I'm looking for. Its not hard, once you been involved with a breed for a long time."

Since awareness of the Marwari and its heritage first began to blossom in India, Francesca says breeders and horse traders are beginning to take better care of their animals.

"Husbandry has really improved in recent years," she says. "People have started getting quite competitive. It's helped people feel that they belong to something, and with government subsidies, the horse has become of value to them.

"It happens slowly, but it happens."

Dilraj, the Marwari Horse
(courtesy Francesca Kelly)

The Friesian

*I*f Elizabeth Taylor was a horse, she would have to be a Friesian. All tossing black locks and prancing poses.

But there's much more to this Netherlands native than just looks. As one of the oldest continuous breeds in Europe, its blood runs through some of our most illustrious equine characters, from the Shire to the Fell Pony.

Yet it's a miracle that this glamorous, hardworking horse is still here. In 1913, after an unbroken line going back to the Roman Empire, there were only three stallions left.

Descended from the European Forest Horse (*Equus caballus sylvaticus*), the Friesian has been the archetypal battle mount for centuries. It was first recorded in AD 150 by Roman historians writing about cavalry assigned to Hadrian's Wall on the border of the Roman Empire with Scotland. Mercenaries using Friesian stallions were also recorded at Carlisle in the 4th century AD.

The Normans with William the Conqueror may well have been riding Friesians at the Battle of Hastings in 1066, and historians wrote of the 'Great Horse' being used for centuries afterwards. In continental Europe, Friesians were ridden to the Crusades and many of the wars of the Middle Ages, particularly once refined with the introduction of Arab and Andalusian blood.

Because they were so striking, Friesians were noticed wherever they went. The German Elector Johan Frederik van Saksen rode a notable Friesian in the 1540s, while a famous etching of 1568 shows a Friesian stallion called Phryso, which belonged to Don Juan of Austria.

In the 17th century, the Friesian was probably a foundation breed for the Old English Black, which was produced in the East of England and eventually became the Shire – though at first it was noted for its bulk and ugliness before being refined by outcrossings. The Friesian also probably contributed to the Fell Pony we know today.

In Europe, the Friesian was not only valued for its strength and capability as a cavalry charger, but was also popular in haute école dressage and carriage driving, often found in Spanish riding schools where it was used with more usual Spanish breeds for classical riding.

However, during the 18th century, the Friesian became limited to its native province of Friesland, its demise possibly linked to the decline of nobility in Europe after the French Revolution. Farmers used it for pulling their gigs to church and for trotting races, sitting on only a small orange blanket instead of a saddle. The Friesian's prowess as a trotter led to it being used to produce the Orlov Trotter and, later, American trotting breeds.

But competition with heavier draught breeds such as the Bovenlander, which was better for the agriculture that was the main industry in the region, almost spelled the end for the Friesian. Despite liking their beauty and gentle nature, farmers couldn't justify keeping a horse that seemed to be better at dancing than pulling a plough.

Then, on May 1, 1879, a group of people decided that something had to be done to save their native horse. They met at a tavern in Roordahuizum and formed a studbook, setting in place many of the rules we see in the breed today.

"In the Middle Ages, there used to be white and brown horses, but when the studbook was created, the breed was defined as just black, with a white star only," says John Ombler of the Friesian

Horse Association of Great Britain and Ireland.

But even though registering the remaining Friesians boosted interest in its breeding, many people still preferred the Bovenlander as a working horse. In 1913, only three old stallions were left in the province, with no younger ones available to take their place.

It could so easily have been the end of the breed.

However, Friesian-lovers were not about to give up. Around 100 people met at the Oranjehotel in Leeuwarden to set up a breed society and plan a course of action to save the beautiful black horse.

In order for it to compete successfully with the Bovenlander, it was bred to be tougher and heavier, sacrificing some of its looks in the process. For a time, that seemed to work – people were so enamoured of the horse's friendly and docile temperament that there were always plenty of them willing to safeguard the breed.

But as with all European horses, the two world wars took their toll, particularly when the Netherlands had to return to horsepower after the Second World War to alleviate a food shortage and the Bovenlander was the obvious choice for field work.

By the 1960s, the Friesian faced another crisis as the world turned away from horsepower and farms became mechanised. Only 500 mares were registered in the Friesian studbook in 1965. It looked like the Friesian was destined to disappear after all.

Luckily the Dutch economy improved, allowing time and money for leisure. People looking for leisure pursuits such as horse riding and carriage driving found that the friendly Friesian with its dancing feet was the ideal choice, particularly if they had never owned a horse before. It had been a close-run thing, but the Friesian began to be bred for dressage and carriage driving again.

Now there are strict controls so the breed doesn't face extinction again, either by neglect or by outcrossing. Cross-breeding with other breeds is forbidden if the owner wants to show or compete their Friesian.

"The Friesian studbook, Koninklijke Vereniging Het Friesch Paarden-Stamboek (KFPS), is one of the most successful stud books in the world," says John Ombler. "Friesians have to be purebred to be recognized by KFPS – there are no Approved Stallions in the UK, indeed very few stallions stand at stud outside Friesland, so breeding has to be by AI [artificial insemination]. Breeding is strictly controlled. Cross-breeding and breeding from stallions that have not been approved is frowned upon, but everyone accepts that it can't be banned – it does happen, even in The Netherlands.

"If 3,000 colts are born, only 10 stallions will be recognized for breeding after a lengthy inspection and testing process – including testing their genes to make sure they don't carry a chestnut gene – their joints are X-rayed for soundness, their semen quality tested…

"Then there is the inspection procedure – 10 weeks training in dressage, driving and aptitude testing. They're known for being very docile, willing horses, so anything crazy wouldn't be accepted."

Now the Friesian is being bred all over the world, and its future looks bright. "Many people in this country still view the Friesian as a heavy, commercial driving horse," says John. "But in The Netherlands they have been trying for some time to develop a finer type, more of a sports horse, more versatile, more athletic. In the UK the Friesian is widely used as a commercial carriage driving horse, but in recent years have started to become recognized as a serious dressage horse, general riding horse and in many cases a loyal family friend. In the Netherlands it is mainly used for dressage."

There are still some of the more stocky, compact Friesians around, since it will take several generations to breed out those characteristics that were desirable in the early 20th century, says John.

A modern Friesian stands at between 15.1 and 16.1 hands high (1.58-1.65m). But while the feathering around the legs, the powerful chest and the arched neck of the traditional horse have been retained as part of the new breed profile, today's Friesian breeders aim for a longer lines, which look better in the show ring. The breed's intelligence and good nature are still an important part of its profile, however.

There are still only a couple of hundred Dutch Friesians in the UK, and there are a few studs now in the UK dedicated to breeding the Friesian in line with the KFPS breeding goals – though a good, well-bred Friesian does not come cheap. Nevertheless, as with other breeds rescued from the brink, a handful of dedicated people ensured that we can all still enjoy the equine Elizabeth Taylor – one of the world's most glamorous horses.

Friesian
(courtesy Friesians Scotland)

Wild and Free

Onaqui herd of wild mustangs in Utah, USA
(courtesy US Bureau of Land Management)

The Tahki

*I*n the stifling gloom of a deep, subterranean cave a horse gallops across a wall into the shadows. Outlined in black charcoal, this horse speaks to us across the centuries; drawn by men who saw it grazing the plains, hunted it with bow and arrow – perhaps even worshipped its wild spirit.

Look closely: it is stocky and short-legged. A dark stripe runs down its back. Its mane stands upright. The archetypal prehistoric horse, extinct in the wild for generations.

Yet you will probably still recognize it – and know it by another name: Przewalski's Horse.

For, unlike the dodo, the passenger pigeon and, just recently, the Yangtze River dolphin, this wild horse from the Mongolian steppe has been bred in animal parks and zoos for more than a century and is one of conservation's success stories. It has even been reintroduced to the Asian steppe and now runs wild and free as its ancestors once did.

Even so, its story could so easily have been one of tragedy rather than triumph. Just another creature erased from the face of the earth in mankind's dismal record.

For all the 'wild' horses roaming the world, only one can truly claim that distinction. The Mongolian wild horse, called the Takhi, or Takh, in its home country, was 'discovered' by Colonel Nikolai

Przewalski of the Imperial Russian Army in 1879.

But though it looks like an early blueprint for the equine companions we know today, it is no ancestor to the domestic horse. It has 66 chromosomes compared to the 64 of domestic breeds, and analysis of mitochondrial DNA (the genetic history of the maternal line) in 1995 showed that the Takhi did not give rise to today's Arabians and Thoroughbreds. And apart from its dorsal stripe, upright mane, and almost non-existent forelock, it differs from domestic horses in that it sheds its mane and tail once a year.

So where did it come from? And what is it?

Well, there is consensus that it is different to *Equus caballus*, the domestic horse, but apart from that, no one really knows how to categorise it. There is even disagreement over its name.

According to Christian Stauffer of the International Takhi Group, the umbrella group of all institutions participating in the reintroduction of the wild horse to Mongolia, "The name is *Equus caballus przewalskii*. It might be considered a subspecies of *Equus caballus*, but this is difficult because no other form is existing."

Dr Patricia Moehlman, chair of the IUCN/SSC Equid Specialist Group, however, cites a 2004 scientific paper in the journal *Animal Genetics* that reports that "the split between *Equus przewalskii* and *Equus caballus* occurred over 100,000 years ago and pre-domestication of the horse. Hence they are considered sister taxa. For now, the official taxonomic designation is *Equus ferus przewalskii*."

Whatever its name, its ancestors probably roamed Eurasia in the Pleistocene and Holocene periods, perhaps alongside the Tarpan (*Equus caballus gmelini* Antonius) or the Forest Horse (*Equus caballus sylvestris*). Our ancestors hunted it, painting its unmistakeable form on cave walls in what is now France and Spain around 20,000 years ago. But as the climate grew warmer and agriculture replaced hunting, the wild horse became a competitor for forage and land. And, as with feral herds today, wild stallions probably had a tendency to break down fences and abscond with the domesticated mares kept for meat. Gradually, the wild herds were pushed further away from settlements, out to lands unsuitable for cultivation.

Eventually, the herds were confined to Central and Southeast Asia, but because the Mongolian nomadic tribes also ran their semi-domesticated stock on the steppe, no one was sure whether the horse was, in fact, truly wild. Linnaeus didn't even include it in his grand 18th-century classification scheme, *System naturae*.

Consequently, no one took much notice that the herds were beginning to diminish. And 1969 was the last time that the Takhi was seen in the wild.

In the 19th century, the Polish explorer Colonel Nikolai Przewalski was commissioned by Tsar Alexander II of Russia to explore remote places, and after a journey to Central Asia, reported that he had heard of wild horses roaming the Mongolian steppe. This news caused great excitement, as all wild horses had been believed to be long extinct. On his second trip, he was given the skull and hide of one of these horses by a frontier guard. Then, on his third journey, he saw two herds of Takhi in the Tachin Schara Mountains on the edge of the Gobi Desert. Describing the horse in 1881 for what was believed to be the first time (two European explorers later claimed to have seen them first), Przewalski gave his name to the animal, then believed to be the primitive ancestor of all modern breeds. Unfortunately, his patron, the Tsar, was assassinated in the same year, so never got to see this wonderful new creature.

Przewalski described a small, stocky, dun-coloured horse around 12–14hh, with a thick neck and black dorsal 'eel' stripe. Its black mane stood upright like a zebra's and ended between the ears instead of continuing into a forelock as in the domestic horse. Its black tail was like that of the wild ass, the stock (the top of the tail where it joins the body) being composed of short hairs with longer hair starting lower down, in comparison to the domestic horse, in which long hair begins right at the top. The wild horse lived in herds of five to 15, led by a stallion, and seemed to be able to go for long periods without water. The animals had acute senses of hearing and smell, and were alert but shy.

The news of these exotic creatures running wild in Mongolia

set off a feeding frenzy among animal collectors. The first expedition to attempt this was ordered by wealthy landowner Frederic von Falz-Fein, who owned hundreds of acres near Askania Nova in Russia. He commissioned a dealer to capture some of the Mongolian horses in 1897, but it was too difficult to catch full-grown animals. Two foals were captured the following year, but died shortly afterwards, unable to thrive on the sheep's milk provided by their captors.

By this time, von Falz-Fein was even more determined. Money was no object – indeed, he eventually spent well over 10,000 rubles, a fortune at a time when one ruble would buy 500 pounds of tea. He made arrangements to rear captured foals on the milk of local mares. In 1899, seven wild foals were captured and though three were lost, the others eventually arrived at Askania Nova. One of the male foals and a filly captured the following year were presented to the Tsar, but when the filly died, the Tsar returned the stallion to von Falz-Fein to begin a breeding programme. Two more foals were caught in 1900 and taken to Moscow.

In England, another wealthy landowner had set his sights on obtaining some of the rare horses. The Duke of Bedfordshire was the chairman of the Zoological Society of London, and already had a collection of rare animals at his Woburn estate. He commissioned renowned Hamburg animal dealer Carl Hagenbeck to fetch him some Takhis. Other collectors in Europe and America also demanded their own wild horses.

But in those days, animal collecting was an adventure for those taking part, with no one considering the trauma for the animals being chased and captured. Out of 51 foals captured in 1901 and taken on the first arduous, seven-month trip to Europe, only 28 survived to reach their final destinations – Woburn, New York, Berlin, Halle, Manchester, London, Hamburg, Paris and Gooilust in Holland. Another 14 were captured during the following two years, but were in such poor condition when they arrived that they died shortly afterwards. Today, it's believed that the race to acquire foals of the exotic horse for foreign collections – which sometimes meant killing the adults that tried to defend them – may have even contributed to the horse's swift demise.

Of all the wild Mongolian foals captured during those years, so many died or were unable to breed that only 13 provided the line of descent to today's captive animals. Inbreeding was a huge problem. Many of the horses were kept in small, grassless enclosures, often mating with siblings and parents, and this may have had the knock-on effect of resulting in a shorter lifespan for today's Takhis, along with a high rate of mortality in foals. By the end of the Second World War the world's breeding population was down to only 12.

But there were no more wild herds from which to draw new blood. Several expeditions tried to find them, but increasing pressure from agriculture and development had taken its toll, and the last wild Takhi was seen in 1969 at a spring called Gun Tamga in southwest Mongolia.

The world's last truly untamed horse was extinct in the wild.

The captive population of Przewalski's Horse was also in trouble. By 1977, there were only 300 left worldwide, scattered among zoos and private parks. Pregnancies in mares were decreasing, and when foals were born, they often died before maturity. Then three enthusiasts from Rotterdam then took it upon themselves to start trying to save the wild horse. Setting up the Foundation for the Preservation and Protection of the Przewalski Horse, they established a studbook and began a programme to encourage exchange of Takhis between zoos to prevent any further inbreeding. The foundation's main aim, however, was to start reintroducing the horse to the wild.

In 1981, the foundation began buying Takhis from zoos, and in 1988, in conjunction with the Moscow Academy of Science's Institute of Evolutionary Animal Morphology and Ecology, negotiated to use an area of Mongolian steppe for the breeding programme. The natural grassland known as steppe is itself endangered by overgrazing by agricultural stock or development, and only a few areas in Mongolia are still natural. About 100 km from the capital, Ulan Bator, Hustain Neruu National Park consists of 24,000 acres of grassland and mountain forests. Working with the Mongolian Association for Conservation of Nature and

Environment, the foundation released the first captive-bred Takhis into the Hustain Huruu reserve in 1990.

Another project, initiated by German businessman Christian Oswald and named Takhin Tal, began introducing Takhis to the Gobi-B Strictly Protected Area in western Mongolia in 1992.

But behind the successful reintroductions lie stories as murky as those relating how Przewalski's Horse became extinct in the first place. Rumours abound of infighting between groups racing to be the first to reintroduce the Takhi to Mongolia, and between countries sending the horses from zoos – sometimes more for political expediency than from true conservation concern. There has long been disagreement about how and where to release the Takhi, and how to manage the reintroductions. Some groups said it should go back to the grassland of the central Mongolian steppe, pouring scorn on others that claimed that the scrubland of the Gobi Desert is its true home.

There were setbacks and mistakes in the first years: in the Takhin Tal project, only one pre-release enclosure was provided in which to acclimatise new arrivals, but this allowed one stallion and his harem to keep rivals away from the best vegetation and water; and all foreign researchers were admonished by the Mongolian government in 1993 for over-zealous behaviour. Since then, however, releases have become easier, and several foals have been born and raised in the wild. Dr Moehlman says things have now settled down: "There are three reintroduction sites and they are all working well together."

The name Takhi means 'spirit' or 'spiritual' in Mongolian, and that is a fitting name for an animal that the local people cherish so much. Mongolia has a rich history of nomadic tribes – Genghis Khan's mounted horsemen and their descendants conquered half the known world during the 12th and 13th centuries to build the largest empire in history. Even today, more than a million people live a nomadic lifestyle, moving their herds of livestock across the steppe according to season. And that's a big problem for the Takhi, since it can successfully breed with the domestic horse, producing a hybrid that has 65 chromosomes. If the hybrid then breeds with domestic horse, the offspring has 64 chromosomes, the same as a domestic horse, and looks more like the horse with which we are familiar, rather than the Takhi. Thus, without strict controls, the Takhi could easily become extinct again, simply by interbreeding with domestic horses.

Another problem is the harsh conditions of the steppe. Along with constant winds, summer can bring temperatures as high as 40°C (104°F), while winter may see temperatures drop to −46°C (−50°F), as well as storms of freezing sleet called *dzguds* every five or so years, which kill thousands of animals. Under such conditions, horses can be weakened and become susceptible to wolf predation and infections such as strangles and the tick-borne piroplasmosis.

However, there are encouraging signs that Takhi populations around the world are growing, filling the niche in the steppe ecosystem once occupied by the horse's ancestors. There are ups and downs – only 48 were left after 2010's winter, but 12 foals were born in the Takhin Tal reserve in 2011.

In Hungary, Takhi graze the grassland known as the *puszta*, and researchers hope the wild horse may find a place grazing wildlife reserves – there are even some on forests in Britain. There is still a long way to go before the Takhi is considered out of danger, but the story of how it galloped back from the abyss is surely an inspirational example of what can be done with international cooperation.

The Takhi
(courtesy International Takhi Group, www.savethewildhorse.org)

The Mustang

It is the symbol of frontier America: a herd of wild horses galloping across the plains, manes and tails flying in the wind. It also represents the history of this huge continent, and how it was won – from Spanish Conquistador to painted warrior, bluecoated soldier to hardy cattleman. Without the horse, America might still be wilderness.

But the wild mustang, that potent symbol of freedom, has been under threat since the first horses broke free from the Spanish explorers, and even today, it is in constant conflict with the very people it helped to settle this land. Today it has many champions fighting on its behalf. but only 50 years ago, it seemed as if the mustang would be harried, captured, harassed, tortured and exterminated from the plains it had made its home.

One woman was determined to prevent this happening. And she wasn't about to let the powerful American government get in her way.

There was a horse roaming the western plains of North America 50 million years ago, long before it graced the rest of the world. This was Hyracotherium (formerly known as Eohippus, the Dawn Horse), a small mammal with four-toed front feet and three toes on its hind feet. Eventually, this early horse migrated to Asia across the Bering land bridge from Alaska to Siberia, spreading across Europe and Africa. But in its original home, once humans had arrived – probably across the same land bridge – the horse was hunted for its meat and pelt so extensively that, by the time the Spanish explorers arrived, it had been extinct for around 8,000 years. It has become well documented that, when the Conquistadors first rode into the New World, the native people thought man and horse were joined in one magical being.

Legend has it that Christopher Columbus took hardy Sorraia-type horses on his voyage across the Atlantic. He was intending to take noble Andalusians and breed them along the way, but found at the last minute that someone had substituted the native horses, which retained their ancestral characteristics. This, however, turned out for the best, as the horses were able to withstand the rigours of the voyage and the hardship of the exploring life.

Other ships brought the finest Spanish horses, which had been carefully bred for many years in their home country and served as mounts for gentlemen. They were highly prized across Europe for their beauty, athleticism, intelligence and gentle nature. Stud farms were set up in the Caribbean, from where the horses were imported into Mexico and then into what is now the United States.

In the ships destined for the New World, the valuable horses were kept in the holds, held in slings that allowed them to take the weight off their feet and move with the roll of the ship. Even so, many horses died en route; it's said the Horse Latitudes in the Atlantic gained their name from the numbers of dead horses being thrown overboard. Once the ship had anchored, the horses were blindfolded and carefully lifted out of the holds by hoist and sling, and lowered into the water to swim ashore, led by small boats.

When the Pueblo Indians forced the Spanish out of New Mexico in the late 1600s, many horses were left behind. But though the Pueblo did learn to ride, they mainly valued the horse for meat, and for trading with plains Indians for buffalo hides and meat. It was the plains tribes whose lives were gradually transformed by the horse. The number of horses became a measure of wealth; wars were waged over them, and the balance of power shifted in favour of mounted tribes who could hunt buffalo more efficiently, and therefore had more to trade.

Although northeastern states were settled by northwestern Europeans, who imported their own breeds, by around 1700, Spanish horses were the most common type across the continent, both for riding and as draught animals. They were particularly popular with the Native American tribes, who made stealing them from white settlers an artform.

Huge herds of feral horses were running wild on the plains by now, composed of descendants from horses that had escaped from the Spanish explorers and later colonists. In fact, there were so many 'mustangs', named from the Spanish *mestengo*, stray beast, on the plains, that maps just said 'Wild horses'. By the 19th century the population of wild horses (none were truly wild in the sense of undomesticated Przewalski's Horses, but feral – domesticated horses returned to the wild) had reached an estimated 2 million across 17 western states.

Pureblooded Spanish horses were becoming rare, however, particularly once the last native tribes were decimated and their horses shot or confiscated. In many feral herds, the stallions were killed and replaced with males from larger breeds in an attempt to obtain larger animals (the true Colonial Spanish Horse only stands around 14hh). Most wild horses have been crossed over the years with non-Spanish horses, and are often considered to be of little value because they were too small for European-Americans, and because of their association with the Indians and Mexicans. In the First World War, more than a million were taken to the Front Line. Until as recently as the 1970s, wild horses could be captured and turned into horsemeat for dogs, chickens or humans. This latter fate still awaits hundreds of wild horses each year– but at least their methods of capture are a little more humane, and they have more advocates, thanks to an unassuming woman nicknamed Wild Horse Annie.

Velma Bronn was born in Reno, Nevada, in 1912, the oldest of four children. There was a thrilling tale in the family's history that seemed to resonate through Velma's own destiny: her father, Joseph was said to have been raised on the milk of a mustang mare as his parents crossed the deserts in a covered wagon. When he grew up, he ran a freighting business that used horses descended from mustangs.

Like many youngsters in the West, Velma grew up around horses on the family ranch, but at the age of 11 she contracted polio and was forced to spend six months in a cast in a San Francisco hospital. She said later that being confined and in pain like this made her appreciate the suffering of captured animals all the more. Her face disfigured by the disease, she was taunted at school, so ploughed her energy into her schoolwork and in looking after animals on her family's ranch near Wadsworth, Nevada. When she eventually married their strapping, six-foot-four neighbour, Charlie Johnston, he took over the running of the ranch. Velma worked as an executive secretary for a Reno insurance firm.

When she was driving to work one morning in 1950, a livestock truck cut in front of Velma's car. There was blood streaming from it. Aghast, Velma followed the truck to a rendering plant, where she hid behind a shrub and saw something that would change her life forever. The truck was crammed full of wild horses, and a yearling that had fallen down between two stallions was being trampled to death in the panic because the horses could not move enough to get out of the way.

Like many western Americans, Velma had been vaguely aware that wild horses were being captured on the range, but she had never thought much about it. Now, as she wrote later: "...my own apathetic attitude was jarred into acute awareness. What had now touched my life was to reach into the lives of many others as time went on." She became determined to find out more.

What she discovered shocked and horrified her so much that she knew she had to put a stop to it. Hundreds of wild horses and burros (donkeys) were run down by planes – often piloted by men who had recently flown in the Second World War – until they fell from exhaustion. Then men following in trucks and on horseback would rope them, fixing wires around their noses to partially close their nostrils so they couldn't breathe properly and regain their energy, and tie heavy truck tyres to the ropes to weigh the horses down until a livestock truck could catch up. Then the animals would be packed tightly into the trucks without food and water and taken to rendering plants to be converted into chickenfeed and dog food. Others were chased on horseback and with trucks into corrals and shot at close quarters; many were shot on the range and left to die (see Marilyn Monroe's movie *The Misfits* for a better idea of these methods).

Velma began publicising these practices and collecting signatures opposing them. She urged children to write to congressmen; she gave presentations to businessmen, schools and townspeople across her home county of Storey. Her first victory came two years later when she organized the presentation of a petition to the Storey County Board of Commissioners with 147 signatures, protesting an application for a permit for hunting wild horses by aircraft. Velma showed the board photographs of bleeding wild horses crammed into trucks. The board consequently banned the use of aircraft to spot and chase down wild horses.

But Velma was not content to stop at a local campaign. Three years later, she and her supporters succeeded in getting a similar ban passed across the whole of Nevada – except for public lands, which made up more than 80 percent of the state. Public lands are administered by the federal US government, and consist of millions of acres across the country.

Still Velma fought on, gaining support from the public and influential people bit by bit. Then, during a heated public meeting in Virginia City, an irate dissenter called her "Wild Horse Annie". Although the term was meant to be derisory, the press pounced upon it, and the campaign flooded across America, fuelled by an intensive letter-writing campaign by children to newspapers and politicians. The whole country was outraged as the facts of wild horse capture and treatment were made public, prompting The Associated Press to write that it was very unusual for an issue to receive so much public attention nationwide and touch "such a responsive chord".

In 1959, Nevada Congressman Walter Baring introduced a bill banning the use of all motorised vehicles to hunt down wild horses on public lands, as well as polluting waterholes to trap them. The House of Representatives passed it unanimously, and the 'Wild Horse Annie Act' became law on September 8, 1959.

Surely now the American mustang would be free to roam across the West, reoccupying the niche left vacant by its ancestors?

No: Velma soon realised that however tempting it was to celebrate victory after the long years of campaigning, the fight was not yet won. The bill had not incorporated her recommendation that the wild horse population be managed sustainably and protected from private hunters – and, even worse, there was no enforcement of the new law. In her own home state, for example, the law was openly flouted with a roundup of wild horses for slaughter – yet Velma was unable to get those responsible convicted.

For the next 10 years, despite her husband's death from emphysema, Velma intensified her campaign. Only the Vietnam War generated more letters to Congress. The International Society for the Protection of Mustangs and Burros was formed by John and Helen Reilly in 1960; Velma, who served as its first president, and her assistants made meticulous notes on all the herds of wild horses they could find, including maps, photos, witness statements and other documents. The society also succeeded in getting several refuges established where wild horses could roam without fear of being captured; the largest, established in 1966, being on the huge Nellis Air Force Base in Nevada. The Pryor Mountain Wild Horse Refuge on the Wyoming-Montana border was established in 1968, and in a unique agreement with the federal Bureau of Land Management (BLM), Velma found homes for some orphaned mustangs – beginning a programme of adoption that was eventually taken over by the BLM in 1976 and became the agency's Adopt a Horse/Burro programme that is still in effect today.

Eventually, facing more than 70 bills demanding protection for wild horses, both houses of Congress passed The Wild Free-roaming Horse and Burro Act of 1971, which provided for management and control of the animals on public lands. President Richard Nixon signed it into law. The act states that:

"...wild free-roaming horses and burros are living symbols of the historic and pioneer spirit of the West; ...they contribute to the diversity of life forms within the Nation and enrich the lives of the American people."

The act bans the use of motorised vehicles or aircraft to chase or capture wild equines. Amendments in 1976 and 1978 lent teeth to the first law, allowing for the adoption of wild horses by the public under federal supervision, and permitting helicopters to be used by federal employees to manage the herds, since this is still said to be the least-stressful way of rounding up the horses ready for adoption.

But the mustang's champion, living with her mother at the family ranch, was not to see the benefits of her life's passion. Though she had survived bitter vitriol and even threats on her life, in 1977 she succumbed to cancer at the age of sixty-five.

Karen Sussman, third president of the International Society for the Protection of Mustangs and Burros (ISPMB), worked closely with Velma's secretary, Helen Reilly, and says the campaign for the 1971 act was driven by Velma's strength of will.

"Annie was a magnificent woman. She was well before her time and the women's liberation movement in our country. She pretty much singlehandedly saved the wild horses and burros in our country from elimination. She brought attention to the West, which was dominated by strong cattle interests, and made apparent to the American people that the public lands were for the public, not special interests. To take on the powerful cattle industry was phenomenal in her time. She also was disfigured from polio, and with this handicap, her strong will and her love of the land the West, she made a powerful impact, finally, with the aid of children across the United States.

"The horses are still struggling to survive in our country," Karen adds. "Velma realized the law that she was instrumental in getting passed in 1971 to protect wild horses and burros would be only as good as those people (she called them attitudes) who carried out the law. She realized before she died that the horses would still have a struggle, but she certainly slowed down the process to a point where we may still have time to save them."

She says that there are currently less than half the population of wild horses and burros of 1971, when the law noted that they were fast disappearing. "Cattle interests are still powerful in the West, and many of them dominate the BLM and Congress," she says.

The BLM estimated in May 2006 that there were 32,000 wild horses and burros on its rangelands in 10 states – 4,000 more than it believes can "exist in balance with other public rangeland resources and uses". Just over 11,000 were removed from the range in 2005. Another 26,000 were in short-term or long-term holding facilities awaiting adoption or sale. Ranchers rent grazing on public lands, paying, remarkably, just over $1 for each animal per month (Animal Unit Month – AMU), calculated from a 1966 base rate and adjusted for current beef prices, grazing fees on private land and production costs. The grazing fee for 2012 is $1.35 per AMU. Deer and other game using the lands are "paid for" by hunting licenses. However, no one pays for the grazing wild horses use, so they are not cost-effective. Proponents point to studies showing that horses fill an ancient vacant niche, and that game can survive very well alongside equine herds – it is the cattle and sheep that are overgrazing the range. Opponents say the horses are not wild but feral, so are not a natural part of the ecosystem.

There has been huge scandal as 'adopted' horses have been bought en masse and sold off to slaughterhouses. Although the Wild Horse and Burro Act prohibits the animals being sold for 'commercial products', after a year of adoption, ownership reverts from the government to the adopters, when the horses are no longer considered wild so are not covered by the protection afforded by the 1971 act.

Even as recently as 2005, President George W. Bush signed a federal appropriations bill with a rider attached at the last minute allowing mustangs over the age of 10, or those not adopted after being offered three times, to be sold "to the highest bidder". There was a huge public outcry – no less than from Congressmen who were unaware that they were agreeing to such a law – and the first two sales sent horses to processing plants for human consumption in Europe and the Far East. Consequently, the BLM suspended the sales for a month while it assessed its adoption efforts and tried to reach agreement with the processing plants that they would not accept horses carrying BLM freeze-brands. "Our agency is committed to the well-being of wild horses and burros, both on and off the range," BLM Director Kathleen Clarke says. "Congress placed no limitations or restrictions on the animals purchased. The animals will be classified as private property upon purchase. Our emphasis is to find good homes for the animals."

Despite the government's stance, the mustang's advocates didn't lose heart. The ISPMB contacted people all over the world, including Hollywood celebrities, asking for support in opposing the rider, as well as taking more proactive action: "Our organization is taking an active role in trying to place 8,000 of these animals on Tribal lands where the horses will be held in a conservation program."

In September 2006, the US House of Representatives finally passed the American Horse Slaughter Prevention Act to prohibit the transportation and sale of horses for human consumption. This bill was supposed to stop horses ending up on the table by prohibiting the inspection of plants that butchered horses. Without inspections, the meat could not be sold for human consumption. However, the bill didn't end the slaughter; it just pushed it over the borders to Mexico and Canada.

At the end of 2011, President Barack Obama signed into law a new bill restoring the inspections, ostensibly so that the government could keep an eye on horse export and act if a horse-slaughter plant opened. Many states already ban horse slaughter, but in 2010, more than 140,000 were shipped to other countries for slaughter, many probably ending up on the menu in countries such as France and Japan.

Karen Sussman says the new bill does not go far enough to protect wild horses from destruction. "Congress removed the protections that prohibit the wanton slaughter of thousands of horses thus putting 36,000 wild horses, held in pastures in the Midwest, at risk of inhumane destruction. We cannot let that happen. Wild horses are our heritage. They are the living embodiments of our freedom. They are too precious to lose."

She vows that the ISPMB will continue to fight to stop the

export of live horses and the slaughter of wild horses.

Now others have taken up Velma Johnston's baton, but the wild horse question raises just as much passion on both sides as when she began her campaign in the 1950s. Where ordinary people see spirits of the wild and symbols of freedom and the settling of America, ranchers see vermin that compete for precious grazing land.

But more and more people are taking up the cause, in particular highlighting the genetic diversity of some herds. Many populations have genes from old Spanish lines or are even relatively purebooded, and some represent an important stock of genes found nowhere else in the country.

"Right now, wild horses are genetically far more diverse compared to any breed of horse in our country," says Karen Sussman. "That means there is very little inbreeding in wild horses, whereas some of the domestic breeds are in real trouble. The reason that wild horses have this great genetic diversity is because the ratio of stallions to mares is around 40:60 or even 50:50. We should learn something about that.

"However, in 10 more years' time, if the special interests have their way and we keep the same Congress, the future of wild horses and burros will be in jeopardy in our country. Right now, the government has limited or reduced numbers to the point where the wonderful genetic diversity that these horses carry will be compromised."

Other Wild Horses

The Colonial Spanish type
Despite a concerted attempt by earlier governments to wipe them out, some pockets of pure Spanish horses can still be found today on the North American continent. They are considered an important repository of Colonial Spanish genes, since horses in modern Spain have been cross-bred for centuries and are now very different to their ancestors that conquered the New World from 1540 to 1821.

The Sulphur Herd Management Area in southwest Utah is along the Old Spanish Trail from Los Angeles, California, to Santa Fe, New Mexico, which was used by traders and explorers for many years. Furs from Utah and woollen blankets from Mexico were carried to California and traded for horses and mules. But these caravans were often waylaid on their return trip and the precious Spanish horses stolen. Chief Walkara of the Utes was notorious for this, and in 1840, had the distinction of being behind the biggest horse-stealing raid in history.

With mountain man Peg-leg Smith, Chief Walkara masterminded the theft of more than 3,000 of the finest Spanish horses from missions and ranches all over California. The horses were then driven into the Mojave Desert, hotly pursued by their owners. Resting at a desert spring, the Californians then suffered the further indignity of having their riding horses stolen by Walkara and some of his men who had been hiding in the willows. They were found the following day by more Californians on the trail of the stolen horses, and eventually managed to recapture around 1,200 of them. The rest vanished into the wilds of Utah.

As the ranges were settled by ranchers, the wild horses were largely left to themselves. Some larger domestic stallions were released in an attempt to increase the size of the Spanish horses running wild in the mountains so they could be captured and used on ranches, but these domestic horses and their offspring did not have the hard hooves and overall hardiness of the Spanish horses, and so tended to stay in the valleys, keeping the populations separate. By the 1920s, motorised vehicles had arrived on ranches, and cattle numbers had risen. The wild horse was beginning to be seen as a competitor for the range.

In the 1930s, the US government authorized the removal of the herds from public lands, and 'Mustangers' captured and sold or shot wild horses all across the western states. In Utah, the mixed-blooded valley horses were captured or shot, but a small herd of relatively pureblooded Spanish horses managed to elude capture in the remote Mountain Home Range, which had rugged, steep-sided peaks covered in dense juniper scrub. Even today, this herd has retained its Californian Spanish characteristics, and bloodtyping has revealed a high percentage of genetic markers from Iberian horses.

Other herds of wild horses have small groups of animals with Colonial Spanish ancestry, and some even appear to have ancient Sorraia traits. For example, the herd in the **Cerbat Mountains of Arizona** is being managed by the BLM so that their unique genotype is not swamped by less pure crosses.

Wild herds on **Pryor Mountain** on the Wyoming-Montana border also have Spanish ancestry, and are probably descended from animals owned by the Crow or Shoshone tribes, who kept the bloodlines of their stolen and traded horses pure. The Pryor Mountain horses live in the first refuge established specifically for wild horses.

The first reintroduced horses in **New Mexico** are believed to have been lost by the Spanish explorer Don Juan des Onate, who was searching for the fabled city of El Dorado. The explorer had brought more than 1,500 horses and mules to the continent. In October 1599, a patrol of soldiers was marching to the pueblo (Native American town) of Zuni when it was forced to make camp due to a freak snowstorm. During the night, in the middle of a blizzard, 30 horses broke free from their temporary corrals, and could not be found in the morning, despite intensive searches. More Spanish horses were left to fend for themselves in the wild in the 1600s when European settlers had to flee from Indian attacks.

Historian Carlos LoPopolo of Valencia, New Mexico, established the New Mexico Horse Project after he was asked to look into the rumours that the area's wild horses were descended from the Spanish horses that had escaped from des Onate. An expert on the history of New Mexico during Spanish rule, and a master cartographer, Carlos has researched the genealogies of all the main Hispanic families in the state, and a map he drew of the state during the Spanish period of 1650–1750 was presented to Queen Elizabeth, as well as the Pope, the museum in Mexico City and the Count of Valencia, Spain. Once he began looking closely at the wild horses, he was hooked. The first roundup of wild horses took place in 2000. He and his first wife, Cindy, established the non-profit foundation to find and preserve the remaining horses with Colonial Spanish bloodlines. The project established two reserves, the Campbell Ranch Preserve in the Sandia Mountains, and the Cindy Rodgers LoPopolo Wild Horse Preserve near Escondida, New Mexico. Wild horses roam freely on these reserves, without the threat of adoption or slaughter, and though visitors are welcome, there are strict codes of conduct to be followed so as to cause minimal disturbance to the horses. Cindy died from cancer shortly before the first reserve was opened.

Although there are many wild horses in the Western states, not many still have the Colonial Spanish bloodlines. "All the horses on our preserves are of the stock that we look for and preserve. These horses, except for those that were born on the preserves, have all been rounded up somewhere else in the United States and then transported back to New Mexico. All the horses on the preserves have been tested and compared to other strains. The main thing we use is blood DNA tests done by Dr Gus Cothran of the Equine Blood Typing Research Laboratory at the University of Kentucky. He then tells us which animals to place on the preserves.

"These horses are going away at the rate of one an hour here in the USA," Carlos adds. "They are looked at with distain by both the government and the landowners. Neither the Hispanic ranchers nor the native tribes have any love for them. I would say next to the wolves the wild horse is the most hated creature in the West. It's a shame, but this is why I feel they need to be protected."

Carlos believes that the Colonial Spanish link will only be accepted if it is established using scientific methods, so with the help of archaeologists, the project is now testing DNA from the bones of the region's horses from around the Spanish period. The results will be compared to blood collected from wild horses on the preserves to see how many genetic similarities remain.

Dr Cothran has been involved with the New Mexico Horse Project since its inception, and has conducted bloodtyping on many wild horses in the West, as well as other breeds around the world. "Some of the New Mexico horses do show evidence of Spanish ancestry," he says, "although a full analysis has never been done. What this means is that by comparison with the modern breeds of Iberian ancestry, these horses have molecular genetic characteristics that are consistent with them having Spanish heritage."

However, he cautions that it is not a straightforward case of direct inheritance down the centuries. Even possessing Colonial Spanish genes "does not prove direct Spanish descent nor purity. But at least for some, the genetic markers present are more likely to come from old Spanish blood than from more recent North American breeds where certain markers present in the New Mexico horses are rare or absent. This all really needs more work, so do not believe all that you see. But there is evidence of old Spanish heritage."

The Colonial Spanish horses are only around 14hh, with Roman noses and well-developed muscles. Their cannon bones are often rounded in cross-section, rather than having a flat posterior surface, as in most other breeds. Their manes, tails and forelocks are long but remain largely unmatted. "There are very few wild populations that have strong evidence of old Spanish blood," Dr Cothran says. "Ones that do should be preserved because they represent something that is part of the diversity of the horse that has been lost elsewhere."

Professor D. Phillip Sponenberg of the Virginia-Maryland Regional College of Veterinary Medicine, an expert on equine genetics, has also studied the Colonial Spanish type in great detail, as well as other wild horses. "Colonial Spanish horses are of great historic importance in the New World, and are one of only a very few genetically unique horse breeds worldwide," he says. "The combination of great beauty, athletic ability, and historic importance makes this breed a very significant part of our heritage."

However, he, too, cautions that Colonial Spanish heritage cannot be determined solely on the basis of DNA or bloodtyping, since some cross-bred horses may have a preponderance of Iberian genetic markers, while purebred Colonial Spanish horses may not. In addition, Colonial Spanish horses have a greater variety of blood types than any other single breed in North America. "Bloodtyping and DNA typing are both critically valuable and important adjuncts to conservation programs," he says, "but must be used wisely for the sort of information they provide.

They are not a panacea for the difficult and subjective challenges that face conservationists interested in Colonial Spanish horses. Neither of these techniques is powerful enough to direct conservation programs without attention to overall conformation and breed type as well as historical data. All horses (in the New Mexico Horse Project) are bloodtyped, but unfortunately, the bloodtype information is taken as revealing the proportion of Spanish breeding in an individual horse – and bloodtyping cannot do this."

Carlos LoPopolo, however, is in no doubt about the horses' heritage and his own motivation for preserving them. "They are the closest thing we have to a Native American horse," he says, "a horse upon which this country was built."

Banker ponies in North Carolina

On the barrier islands of the Shackleford Banks off the coast of North Carolina, wild horses gallop along windswept beaches and marshy shores just like they have done for more than 400 years. The Conquistadors explored the coast of North Carolina in the 1500s, bringing their sturdy little Barb horses, probably bred in the Spanish colony of Puerto Rico. Hardy and swift, yet elegant, the horses were descended from those bred on the Barbary coast of North Africa, and were ideally suited for the harsh conditions of the New World. However, conflict with the region's original inhabitants resulted in the Spanish having to flee to their Florida colonies, leaving behind their cattle, pigs, sheep, and the valuable horses.

More Spanish horses arrived on the Outer Banks – barrier islands just off the coast – over subsequent years, swimming ashore from ships headed to the English colonies. Sir Richard Grenville bought stallions and mares, along with tack, from Spanish trading posts on the way to Sir Walter Raleigh's colony at Roanoke in 1585. By the time the English historian John Lawson visited North Carolina between 1700 and 1711, the horses had become naturalised. The Native Americans looked after them with great care, feeding them maize, but never rode them, only using them occasionally to carry a hunted deer carcass back to the village. When agriculturalist Edmund Ruffin visited in 1858, however,

European settlers had taken over the Corolla area and were using the horses on farms and also on the beaches, where they hauled nets in from the sea, along with anyone in trouble on the water. The wild horses were rounded up twice a year so that some could be selected for training.

In recent years, vets at the University of Kentucky conducted DNA testing and confirmed that the horses of the Currituck Outer Banks are, indeed, of Spanish ancestry and, due to their isolation over the past few centuries, they have become a breed in their own right. Some of the other Outer Banks barrier islands off the Carolinas are home to wild horses, sometimes known as Banker Ponies; these include Ocracoke, Hatteras and Shackleford, but the herds are a mixture of breeds and numbers are kept low.

Assateague Island National Seashore

Most wild horses live west of the Rocky Mountains, unknown by the majority of people; but a barrier island off the Southeast coast hosts a famous group that takes part in a major public spectacle each year.

Assateague Island is divided by a fence – on the Maryland side is a herd of Colonial Spanish-type horses grazing the national seashore, while the Virginia half has feral horses on the Chincoteague National Wildlife Refuge. Despite romantic legends concerning pirate ships and wrecked Spanish galleons, the accepted story of their ancestors' arrival on the island is that they were taken there in the late 17th century by their owners, who were trying to avoid livestock taxes and fencing laws.

Although the horses are fairly small, around 12-13hh – and are often called ponies because of their small stature – it is believed that this is due to their poor diet. They have bloated bellies from drinking twice as much water as mainland horses to counteract the saltiness of their food – saltmarsh plants such as cordgrass and American beach grass, as well as bayberry and seaweed. Both herds are kept at around 150 animals so as not to damage their fragile environment of dunes, grasses and saltmarsh.

The Virginia horses are owned and managed by the Chincoteague Volunteer Fire Company. Each July, the horses are rounded up by 'Saltwater Cowboys' and swum across the Assateague Channel to

Chincoteague Island at low tide for a three-day festival, during which the foals are auctioned off. The Pony Penning, as the event is called, or the Chincoteague Pony Swim, was first held in 1924 as a way to raise money for the volunteer fire company. The Pony Swim and associated carnival has been held every year since, except for 1942 and 1943, during the Second World War, and now it's a major attraction, drawing thousands of visitors. Each animal sells for between $1,000 and $2,000, but can reach more than $10,000.

The Maryland herd also has an adoption programme, which helps to keep the numbers to a level that won't damage the national seashore, but the National Park Service, which owns and manages the herd, also darts the mares with a contraceptive. The vaccine stimulates the immune system to produce high levels of antibodies, which prevent fertilization.

Sable Island, Nova Scotia, Canada

Sable Island is a sand bar around 160km off Nova Scotia, Canada. According to the Sable Island Green Horse Society, the island, which measures a mere 42km by 1.5km, is the windiest place in the province of Nova Scotia, with the most fog and the least sunshine. Yet the island is home to a between 200 and 350 wild horses.

The Sable Island herd is descended from animals brought to the island in the 1700s and 1800s. However, unlike most of the other populations of wild/feral horses, the Sable Island herd is not managed: the horses are left to fend for themselves in their own society – albeit under the curious gaze of researchers. Since 1961, they have been protected by the Canadian government.

The horses, along with a plethora of other species (though no other mammals) live in a world of sand dunes, ponds, heathland and beaches – and only one tree. Yet they have been thriving for centuries without human interference. But this wild paradise is under threat, as the government of Canada ponders whether to close the lifesaving station on the island, thus ending a permanent human presence after 200 years.

North Dakota Badlands

On a ranch in the Little Missouri Badlands of North Dakota run wild horses that, at first glance, may seem similar to others roaming the Western states. But what makes these Nokota horses special is their provenance. Many believe that they are descended from horses owned by the great Sioux Chief Sitting Bull, some of which were present at the Battle of the Little Bighorn.

When Theodore Roosevelt National Park was established near Medora, North Dakota, in the 1950s, a handful of bands of wild horses were enclosed within its fences. Park administrators tried to get rid of them. During the 1970s, however, due to public pressure, the park modified its policy, recognizing that the horses were part of the state's history and therefore worth conserving – particularly since President Theodore Roosevelt, for whom the park was named, was a keen historian and rancher who had once lived in the area and even seen the horses, writing that they were just as wild as the pronghorn antelope of the plains. However, in the 1980s, order to improve the appearance of the horses, which were small and often pinto or other 'paint' colours, domestic bloodlines were introduced. The herd was thinned out, and since the National Park Service (NPS) had successfully fought to be excluded from the Wild Horse Annie Act of 1959 and the 1971 Wild Free-roaming Horse and Burro Act, that meant that there were no regulations preventing the horses from being sold for slaughter.

Local ranchers Leo Kuntz Jr. and his brother, Frank, were intrigued by the tales attached to the wild horses and started buying up as many as possible before they were slaughtered. Researching their history, they discovered that the horses belonging to Sitting Bull and his warriors had been confiscated upon their surrender at Fort Buford, North Dakota, in 1881. The Sioux chief and his followers had taken refuge in Canada after the Battle of the Little Bighorn, the great victory over General George Custer in 1876. But it was clear from the reprisals after the defeat of Custer's Seventh Cavalry that the old ways were dead, and there would be no permanent asylum for them anywhere.

Most of the herds were dispersed, but 250 of the horses were sold to the Marquis de Mores, a French businessman who ranched in the Little Missouri Badlands and founded the town of Medora, named after his American wife. He sold 60 of the mares to the large HT Ranch, which cross-bred them to obtain saddle horses and polo ponies. Some of the Sioux horses bore old scars from bullet wounds probably suffered in fights such as the Battle of the Little Bighorn. Although many had the characteristics of Colonial Spanish horses, the Sioux animals were heavier and more robust, probably due to the influence of the Canadian Horse, developed over the border from Norman and Breton horses. The uncommon blue roan is a dominant colour in the Nokota. Sitting Bull emphasised the heavy shoulders and feathered fetlocks in his drawings; the humans are practically stick figures, yet you can see every speckle on the horses' coats.

After setting up the Nokota Breed Registry in 1999, the Kuntzes have concentrated on maintaining the old bloodlines, allowing the horses to run free on their ranch near Linton, while trying to get the NPS to reinstate the old Nokota bloodlines in Theodore Roosevelt National Park, instead of the modern Quarter Horse crosses. The Nokota has even been declared the Honorary State Equine by the state legislature (government) – the only state horse in the US.

Abaco Barbs

The Spanish explorers did not only bring Colonial Spanish horses to the New World: they also brought Barbs taken to Spain from Africa's Barbary Coast by the Moors. Some of these horses either escaped – or were taken – to Great Abaco island in the northern Bahamas, where their descendants have survived for 500 years – just. In the 1960s, a road was built through the island, allowing access to the pine forests for logging. The horses became targets. People ran them down with trucks to the point of exhaustion, and dogs brought in to control wild pigs went after foals. The horses were slaughtered by the dozen, until, by the early 1970s, there was only one stallion and two mares left on the entire island.

Fortunately, the two mares were on land owned by a sympathizer, former Senator Edison Key. He said later that when his family went to clear the land for the Bahama Star Farm, "we found carcasses and bones everywhere. I started thinking, it just wasn't right." He and a handful of locals captured the two mares and put them in a corral on the farm, along with a stallion brought up from the Marsh Harbor area. The three wild horses were kept and bred until the population had risen to 12. Then they were released.

In 1992, Mimi Rehor from Miami, Florida, sailed across to Great Abaco and encountered the horses. Their numbers were declining again, and she decided to commit herself to preserving them. To this end, she set up the Abaco Wild Horse Fund, managed by Arkwild Inc., a non-profit organisation, dedicated to raising funds and awareness to preserve the remaining horses. When DNA tests concluded that the horses had Barb heritage, Mimi changed the name of the fund to the Abaco Barbary Horse Project, and the Horse of the Americas Registry accepted the horses as a separate breed descended from Spanish ancestors – although some local residents believe the horses were brought to the island by loggers only in the 1920s.

In 2004, the Bahamas Government set aside a sanctuary for the horses in the pine forest, but by 2012 their numbers had fallen to five. Mimi is currently trying to raise funds for their removal to a US university that specialises in equine reproduction.

Australian Brumbies

Brolgas and roos, squirrels that fly; the *Man From Snowy River* – is there anywhere else on earth as exotic and romantic as Australia? And to an outsider, one creature conjures up the wild, free Outback more than any other: the brumby.

Like the mustang in America, the brumby is a domestic horse gone back to the wild. And, also like the mustang, it is regarded by authority and agriculture as a pest, to be eradicated as quickly as possible. The origin of the name has many stories, each with its own group of supporters. One theory is that it comes from the Aboriginal word for wild, *baroomby*. Another is that it actually derives from a man called Brumby.

The first horses arrived in Australia in 1788 with the First Fleet of convicts from Britain. Then, with the Third Fleet in October 1791, came the newly formed New South Wales Corps, part of the 102nd Regiment, destined to replace the marines who were keeping order in the colony and had been there from the outset. Among the soldiers on the ship Britannia was Private James Brumby from Scotton, Lincolnshire, who had only enlisted the year before. Ambitious and capable, James Brumby, along with other soldiers, was granted land, and by 1794, he owned 12 acres at Hunters Hill. By 1797, however, this grant had been cancelled. Instead, together with three other privates, he owned 100 acres at Mulgrave Place, where he grazed cattle and horses, as well as on government land. In 1801 he had become a sergeant, and three years later, he was posted to Tasmania to become part of a new settlement. Some of his horses were roaming semi-wild on his Australian land and could not be 'mustered', or rounded up, in time, so they had to be left behind. Gradually, they became known to the locals as Brumby's horses; later, simply as brumbies.

Like the American mustangs, the brumby has fought a constant battle with the authorities for the right to roam the wilderness, but until recently has found few supporters. Then, in 2000, 600 brumbies were shot from government helicopters in Guy Fawkes River National Park, many being left to die from their wounds. The RSPCA successfully sued, charging cruelty, and the incident galvanised the Australian public, with millions of people petitioning the government for protection for these creatures that symbolise everything Australia stands for.

Neighbouring New Zealand has the Kaimanawa, a once feral horse, and its preservation is also in the hands of the general public.

There's still a long way to go before the mustang is accepted as part of natural ecosystems, but its advocates are vocal and increasing all the time. Academic studies are showing that wild horses are simply filling niches left vacant by their ancestors.

However, if it wasn't for an unassuming woman from Nevada who stood up to be counted in the 1950s, there might not be any wild horses left to protect. If she could see how her cause has blossomed and been taken up by so many people, so that the issue of wild horses has become a major point of contention in modern politics, there's no doubt she would be amazed – but delighted.

Mustangs in Utah
(courtesy US Bureau of Land Management)

The Carneddau Pony

High on the rugged moorland of Snowdonia, North Wales, grazing on whatever rough foliage he can find, lives a small, shaggy pony carrying an immense heritage on its back. His face was known to the Celts and possibly the Britons before them; his descendants now grace paddocks and stables all over the world. Yet on these high barren peaks, where the wind is a solid force and humans are cowed, the Carneddau Mountain Pony still tosses his head at the comforts of domesticity and gallops free. He is, in the words of one of his champions, "a beautiful survivor in Britain's Jurassic Park".

The Carneddau (the Welsh plural form for "the cairns" and pronounced roughly "carn-airth-eye"), encompass 21,000 acres of some of the wildest land in the UK. There are seven of the highest peaks in Wales – including Tryfan, where Sir Edmund Hillary trained for Everest – and the largest area of continuous ground over 3,000 feet in both Wales and England. Because of their altitude, the peaks support only dwarf shrubs, lichen and woolly hair moss, along with a few other species of vegetation. At lower altitudes are various important habitats such as montane heath, blanket bog, dry heath and bilberry, unimproved acid grassland and rush pastures. Rare species of invertebrate and bird can be found here, including the Chough, which feeds on insect larvae in the short grass and in the dung of the ponies that roam wild over the mountains.

It was here in this magnificent, forbidding wild country of mountains, bogs and lakes, that Prince Dafydd ap Gruffydd was captured with his family in 1283 by the army of King Edward I of England, bringing Welsh independence to a close.

Dafydd was the grandson of Llywelyn Fawr, Llywelyn the Great, who ruled Wales for forty years. He was involved in many bloody campaigns both against his brothers and with them against England in the struggle for control of Wales. At Easter 1282, finally reconciled with his brother Llywelyn ap Gruffydd, Prince of Wales, Dafydd attacked Hawarden Castle, Flintshire, sealing both the fate of his country, and of himself – King Edward was so outraged by what he saw as the betrayal of his crown by a former ally, particularly at such a holy time, that he devised the crime of high treason for Dafydd and countless others after him.

Llywelyn was killed in December of that year and Dafydd succeeded him, but it was a short-lived reign. He and his followers took refuge in the inaccessible mountains of Snowdonia, which had kept the English at bay for so long, and it was there that he himself was betrayed. The following June, while sheltering with his family in a secret hiding place in the bog of Nanhysglain, Dafydd was captured along with his wife, two sons and seven daughters. He was taken to Shrewsbury where he became the first prominent person to be hanged, drawn and quartered.

Dafydd's niece, Gwenllian, only child of Llywelyn ap Gruffydd, was only a baby when her father died, but even though she was so young, she was considered enough of a threat to the English crown that she was captured and spirited away to a convent at Sempringham, Lincolnshire. Here she was kept prisoner until she died aged 54, hidden from the world and prevented from marrying and producing sons who might challenge Edward I for Wales.

But she was not forgotten. As recently as 2009, the mountain Carnedd Uchaf, on the main ridge of the Carneddau range, was renamed Carnedd Gwenllian in honour of the lost Welsh princess.

Gareth Wyn Jones's family have farmed the rocky peaks of the

Carneddau area for 10 generations, and in all that time, the wild ponies have grazed on the hillsides.

"They were here long before us, but we have records that prove they've been on our land for the past 350 years," he says proudly. The ponies are the only wild equine population in the United Kingdom, he adds.

Ponies have been part of the British landscape for thousands of years. The jawbone of a pony was found on the Great Orme, the huge rocky outcrop near Llandudno, and dated to around 10,000 years ago. Gareth believes the Carneddau pony is the direct descendant of the Celtic pony and ancestor of the Welsh Section A pony, and is a unique link to the past.

"The Romans admired the ponies for their strength and agility and used them whilst in Wales and even shipped some of them back to Rome to carry out various tasks on their homeland. In Tudor times King Henry VIII ordered the ponies to be destroyed because they could not carry a knight in full armour, but luckily he did not succeed in wiping them out."

The Carneddau Mountain Pony is similar to the Welsh Section A Mountain Pony, but smaller, standing around 10 or 11 hands high. It is stocky and tough, and incredibly surefooted so it can race across the rocky terrain.

"It is a lot stronger than other ponies; its bones are stronger. It's got some astronomical power for such a little pony."

It also has a thick coat in the winter that protects it even in the harshest weather.

"My grandfather told me that in 1947 half the ponies died in the hard winter when they froze on their feet," says Gareth, "then more died in the winter of 1963. So what we've got left are the strongest of them all. They are really self-sufficient. There's not a lot of forage up there, but they live perfectly well, as high up as 3,000 feet. In the 1970s there was a big snowstorm on the top and the RSPCA tried to put out hay for some ponies that were stuck in a snowdrift. But they didn't even look at it. They just broke through the drift and were off."

Now, because there have been "no hard winters lately to knock them down", he estimates there are between 220 and 240 ponies on the Carneddau massif, managed by his family and other farmers

– though that only consists of keeping an eye on them and bringing them down the mountains once a year to "take off the stallions and old mares and give them a thorough health check". The ponies' numbers have to be reduced each year so the pasture is not overgrazed.

"My great grandfather was a bit of a horse dealer and sold lots of them to the government or to coal mines during the First World War. My father sold some to an American dealer who wanted to set up a herd there. They make fantastic riding ponies. Barry Thomas, the horse whisperer, came up and took a wild one on a Wednesday, and by the Friday his daughter was riding that pony. They're a clean sheet of paper. They haven't been touched by the human hand or learned bad habits, and once they gain your trust, that's something they'll never lose."

Some of the ponies gathered each year are sent to graze conservation areas for organisations such as the RSPB and the National Trust. Native ponies are excellent grazers of land that needs to be protected. They graze and browse selectively, sometimes eating tall grasses, sometimes short, as well as sedges, rushes, gorse and other rough vegetation. They seldom eat flower heads, which allows wild flowers to thrive, but they may trample bracken and brambles and help prevent encroachment by shrub and tree seedlings. Their feeding pattern leaves a mosaic of vegetation that benefits small mammals, birds and insects. Ponies are especially useful in wetland areas where cattle or sheep would trample sensitive vegetation and graze too heavily. In addition, farmers say, native breeds don't need a great deal of management and can survive inclement weather much better than breeds brought in from other areas or foreign countries.

Dave Morris, National Trust Ranger at Bickerton Hill, Cheshire, is in charge of 17 Carneddau ponies that were brought in to graze the precious heathland in 2011 and keep it free of birch saplings that would otherwise take over.

"As we are so close to Wales we thought we would use our local ponies. They are very hardy; they are out all year round and apart from checking their hooves and teeth, annual worming if necessary and a bit of hair cutting, we don't have to do anything with them. Ponies are cheaper to buy than cattle and there's less paperwork."

He says the ponies have retained their wild nature – "some are very shy and always will be, while others are a lot tamer – but I'd rather have them on the wild side so people don't get too close."

In 2007, seven farmers, including Gareth, formed the Carneddau Mountain Pony Association – *Cymdeithas Merlod y Carneddau* – and secured funding and a management agreement in association with the Welsh Assembly Government, the Countryside Council for Wales and the Snowdonia National Park Authority's *Rhaglen Tir Eryri* programme. They were required to bring their sheep down from the mountains during the winter in order to allow the vegetation to recover, and they agreed to continue managing the ponies organically (that is, without medicating or worming them, which might leave chemical residue in their dung that could be passed on to the Chough).

"These mountain ponies are very special to us in Snowdonia," said Rhys Owen, Senior Officer of *Rhaglen Tir Eryri* at the time of the five-year agreement. "Not only do they contribute to our cultural heritage, the Welsh mountain ponies have an important role to play in sustaining the diversity of plants and insects on the mountain slopes. Their grazing patterns mean that they keep vegetation low on the mountain in winter and provide a good source of food to the Chough during the winter. This in turn allows the fragile habitats of the highland to be revitalised when the sheep aren't there."

However, in 2008, when the European Commission adopted a regulation requiring all horses to have microchips and passports, it seemed as if the Carneddau ponies might fade into memory, as they were selling for less than the cost of the passport.

Luckily, the Carneddau Mountain Pony Society managed to obtain a Derogation, or exemption, allowing the ponies to roam on the mountains without having passports and microchips unless they are brought down and sold on to a different area. This helps a bit towards the cost of holding the annual gathering and sale, but stallions still have to be gelded and vets' bills have to be paid. The society would like members of the public to "adopt" a pony to help secure their future. Having them classified as a distinct and rare breed would also help them obtain future funding, Gareth says – though that is a minefield of bureaucracy.

The problem is that that the Carneddau ponies are not recognized by any official body. The Welsh Pony and Cob Society (WPCS), which maintains the stud book for the Welsh breeds, was offered the chance to classify the ponies back in 2004 so they could be managed in a scheme similar to the Hill Pony Improvement Scheme, which covers several herds of semi-feral Welsh Mountain ponies grazing common land around Wales. The hill pony breeders and vets who inspected the herds recommended classification of the Carneddau ponies as a separate type of Welsh Mountain because they had been isolated for hundreds of years, so were probably genetically pure. However, the WPCS declined to accept the Carneddau ponies onto its books because their pedigree could not be traced.

"The Carneddau ponies are not registered Welsh Mountain Ponies or registered Part-breds and I am not sure of the breed origin or indeed their pedigree lineage," says Anna Prytherch, Principal Officer of the WPCS. "They are not recognised in any way by the Welsh Pony and Cob Society and should not be confused with the Welsh breeds. The Carneddau ponies should neither be confused with the Welsh Mountain Section A semi-feral ponies. The semi-feral ponies are all registered with the society and herds are managed on common land across Wales by recognised Hill Pony Improvement Societies."

Consequently, the Rare Breeds Survival Trust and other bodies that might be able to secure funding for their upkeep does not recognize the Carneddau ponies as special.

"The Welsh Mountain ponies recognized as either a rare or as an 'other' native breed by RBST do not include the unregistered Welsh Mountain upland ponies, which I understand are owned by independent Carneddau breeders, as they are not registered animals," says Claire Barber, Conservation Officer of the RBST. "RBST only works to conserve pedigree registered equine breeds, as it is the only way to ensure that we are preserving and maintaining distinct breed genetics. Nor do the Carneddau ponies fulfil our criteria to be recognized as a distinct breed or section of a breed in its own right. RBST, and other organizations like DEFRA (the UK government's Department of Environment, Food and Rural Affairs) and FAnGR (Farm Animal Genetic Resource Committee) do not recognize them as a distinct breed either, and instead they are considered to be unregistered Welsh Mountain ponies.

"The breed that RBST lists as rare (Vulnerable = 500-900 registered adult breeding females) is the Welsh Mountain Section A semi-feral ponies. These are the ponies registered by The Welsh Pony and Cob Society as Section A ponies, which is the foundation for the other sections (B, C and D) in their Stud Book, but which are kept up on the hills and managed in a semi-feral system. RBST currently recognizes these hill ponies as a genetically distinct group to the rest of the animals registered in the Welsh Mountain Section A register (although because of movements of stock between the groups, this is under review).

"RBST uses the following definitions of feral and semi-feral:

Feral populations are defined as a breed which is not subject to routine handling of any kind; and more than 90 per cent of the population have been born to feral parents over two generations.

Semi-feral populations comprise, or are a component of, a recognised native breed that has some level of human input to their husbandry and management.

"For recognition by the RBST a breed must be an original breed, or a native breed of which at least one parent breed is believed to be extinct. Any breed wishing to be recognised should submit a minimum of 25 years (preceding application) of continuous verifiable pedigree data in the form of annual registrations and other documentation.

"As the [Carneddau] ponies are not registered, nor seen or proven to be genetically distinct from other Welsh Mountain ponies, then I do not see it likely that RBST would be able to accept them as a breed on our Watchlist."

So, because the Carneddau ponies have not been registered — for which they need traceable pedigrees — they will not be classified as rare by the WPCS, the RBST or other bodies, which means they can't receive funding from programmes designed to help rare breeds, and could one day disappear as a consequence. It is an endless circle of bureaucracy. It seems that, simply by being allowed to remain wild (or semi-feral, in the definition of the RBST), the ponies don't officially exist as anything except small Welsh ponies living in the mountains – they can't even be treated like other Welsh Mountain hill ponies because they are not registered. Ironically, this alone makes them distinct since they are outside the system.

"I get wound up about it. I think we've got something unique and special, and it's sad that some people haven't the brains to see it," says Gareth.

However, thanks to the efforts of his family and fellow Carneddau owners, more people are becoming aware of the ponies, and the herds are currently the subject of research projects whose results might change their current status.

One long-term project is being run by Dr Susanne Shultz, Senior Research Fellow at The University of Manchester, who is studying the social behaviour of equids such as zebra as well as horses.

"I started working with the ponies for several reasons," she says. "Firstly, they are a unique population of semi-feral ponies and are the closest we have in the UK (and potentially Europe) to understand natural horse behaviour.

"Secondly, horses are really interesting for understanding social behaviour in animals. A lot of focus has been on primates as they are our close relatives. However, horses are interesting not only because they are intensely social, but also because they are so able to form long-term bonds with people. This is likely to be a consequence of their ability to maintain bonded social relationships with each other.

"Thirdly, these ponies are part of Welsh cultural heritage and I hope that our research can help raise their profile and give important information back to the farmers that can help them secure their future. Some of the things we are interested in looking at is the population genetic structure of the ponies, levels of genetic variation between individuals and within the population as a whole."

Another major project, by researchers at Aberystywyth

University, is investigating genetic markers in the ponies' DNA to determine lineage. At the time of this book's publication the results were not yet available, but Gareth is hopeful that they will show once and for all that the Carneddau ponies are unique and should be officially protected.

"We won't give up the fight, even though it can be difficult at times. A couple of lads come up from the village to help us round up the ponies each year but otherwise it's just the families.

"I think we've got the Jurassic Park of Great Britain up here with the only big wild creature that still roams the mountains. They're beautiful and special ponies."

Carneddau ponies
(courtesy Flintshire County Council)

The Sorraia

Dr Ruy d'Andrade had a passion. Not just for one topic: but for fine arts, for architecture, for horse breeding, for zoology, agronomy, archaeology and history. But greater than all of these was his passion for a horse: the ancient Iberian.

He'd first become fascinated with the breed when he'd heard that the Iberian was simply a poor relation of the Arabian. From his extensive knowledge of history, palaeontology and anatomy, this just didn't sound right. He came to believe that this was historically impossible, as well as an unlikely evolutionary outcome. For example, the prehistoric cave paintings of the Iberian Peninsula did not show Arabians, but a different sort of horse altogether.

Then, in 1920, he came across a small herd of semi-wild horses that seemed to have stepped right out of prehistory – and he became determined to search not only for the Iberian horse's ancestor, but to accomplish something much more:

To bring it back.

Ruy was born in Italy in 1880. An architect by profession, he studied agronomy in Pisa and Perugia so he could manage the properties he inherited from his Portuguese father in the Alentejo region of Portugal. He was also a passionate scholar of zoology, anatomy, palaeontology and history, and he'd become an expert on the Iberian horse. He believed that there were two types of horse native to the Iberian Peninsula. A pony, known as Garrano by the Portuguese, or as Asturçone, Navarra, Galego and other names by the Spanish, was a primitive horse of around 12–12.3hh. It was usually bay, with a straight or concave profile and teeth common to most caballine horses.

Today descendants of this pony still live in the north of Spain and northwest of Portugal, east along the Pyrenees as far as the heaths of Cancony. In all this range there is more rainfall and better grass all year round than at lower altitude. Dr d'Andrade believed this small horse had been in the Iberian Peninsula since the mid-Palaeolithic. In 1945 he wrote: "This means that its existence in Iberia is thousands of years old and must still hold almost pure specimens, which amount to approximately 400,000 heads."

The other Iberian horse Dr d'Andrade identified is found in the south of the peninsula, where the climate is more arid. It stands around 14 hh and has teeth more like *E. stenonius*, one of the first wild horse species to reach Eurasia from North America. It was well-known to prehistoric humans, and is also painted on cave walls in the region. These distinctive teeth also occur in some lines of Andalusians. "Teeth, as we know, being among the most common archaeological finds, are the surest and most characteristic element when classifying animals," he wrote. Because of the differences between the teeth of the northern and southern horses, he believed they were different species – or, at least, different subspecies.

In 1920, Dr d'Andrade was hunting in the valley of the River Sorraia in Portugal, when he came across a herd of about 30 unusual-looking wild or semi-wild horses. They were living in dense woods, roaming far and wide and surviving extremes of temperature. Largely unpopulated, the area had formerly been a hunting ground for Portuguese kings and was in the early 1900s under Sesmaria law, which was designed to open up wildernesses for cultivation. The region was used as rough pasture for fighting bulls and livestock, similar to the commons in England. The alluvial soil is sandy, so until the introduction of chemical fertilizers, the region had remained uncultivated.

Many of the horses were mouse-coloured or dun with striped legs, and to Dr d'Andrade's knowledgeable eye, they looked just like probable ancestors of the Andalusian or Lusitano. Similar characteristics were also found in some primitive horses from the Guadalquivir delta region, so he realised that both kinds came from the same ancestral stock. What if these feral horses were actually living remnants of the ancient Iberian?

He determined that he had to save these horses. He later bought a total of 11 horses in the area, carefully selecting individuals that most closely resembled those wild horses he had found, which at that time had disappeared. Some of their characteristics had been dun or 'grullo' (mouse-dun) colour, with a sooty face; withers higher than the croup, giving an 'uphill' profile; a narrow face and a build that reminded him of the wild ass. These horses he installed on his family's land, which had the same kind of terrain they had been used to. Although he had initially selected his horses according to what he believed were closest to the ancestral type, he then allowed nature to take its course, assuming that, as in the wild, the fitter animals would survive. If, after several generations with no outcrosses, the horses bred true to type, then he could be reasonably certain that the animals were, indeed, representative of a pure strain. He named the horse type "Sorraia" from the river valley where he had first seen them.

Not everyone believes that the Sorraia is a direct link to the past. Some claim it to be just a feral horse, mainly because they reject the idea that wild horses could have survived that long in Europe. For the same reason, they deny the English Exmoor that status, although it most certainly represents a primeval form. German hippologist Hardy Oelke, who has studied the Sorraia for years, disputes the idea that the Sorraia is simply the remnant of a man-made breed. He argues that, as well as being a respected scientist, Ruy d'Andrade was an authority on Iberian horses and a breeder of Lusitanos and Andalusians, so would have known if there was an old breed of which the Sorraia was a relic. He also points to tests on mitochondrial DNA (mtDNA, genetic material passed down the maternal line).

"There is no scientific way to prove the status of a subspecies, only circumstantial evidence," Hardy says. "I will say, though, that what we found in the way of mtDNA analyses, combined with the historic facts, is consistent with a status as an indigenous primitive, and ancestral Iberian horse. The theory now is, based on a much larger number of sampled horses, that the Sorraia is an Iberian variant of the Tarpan."

The d'Andrade family still owns many of the descendants of Ruy d'Andrade's herd in a handful of small groups, and another herd was established in Germany in 1974 from some of the original founders during the Portuguese revolution. Studies have shown that there is a lack of genetic diversity in the two populations due to the small number of foundation horses. By 2002, only two maternal lines had survived, and only one paternal line.

Hardy Oelke points out that the fact that the Sorraia has survived the unparalleled inbreeding reinforces the case for the Sorraia being a natural subspecies rather than a man-made breed, that any man-made breed could not have survived such inbreeding. But it was concern about the way the Portuguese treated the Sorraia that spurred him to follow in Ruy d'Andrade's footsteps, he says.

"When I came in contact with the Sorraia and Sorraia owners in Portugal in the early 1990s, its situation there appeared alarmingly threatened in terms of numbers, inbreeding, conditions, situation of their owners, etc., but most of all the inconsistency seen in the attitude of the Portuguese breeders – on the one hand always verbally honouring d'Andrade, on the other hand trampling upon his legacy by their deeds," he says. "They are treating the Sorraia like just another breed, while it is quite obvious that Ruy d'Andrade didn't see it as one. He had no intention to create a new breed, nor did he think he was perpetuating an old one. So I felt compelled to do what was within my limited means to try and help. The inbreeding turned out to be even more intense than I had perceived it to be. Breeders in Portugal generally don't seem to care much about inbreeding, be it Sorraias or Lusitanos. However, by now it is in fact impossible to multiply Sorraias at all without inbreeding, as all living Sorraias are closely related – similar to, but even worse than with, Przewalski's horse."

There may yet be hope for the Sorraia in an unexpected quarter: across the Atlantic. Hardy Oelke is convinced that some bands of wild mustangs in North America, notably the Kiger herd in Oregon and the Sulphur Springs herd in Utah, contain descendants of Sorraias taken to North America by Christopher Columbus, from the Guadalquivir region. These animals were put on the Spanish ships at the last minute instead of the well-bred horses that Columbus had contracted for, but turned out to be better suited for survival in the rough terrain and harsh conditions of the New World.

Hardy has worked hard to promote the idea of Sorraias in the American West, and some people have taken up the cause with gusto – though not always with a thorough understanding of the issues.

"I did not start a 'Sorraia' registry in the US," he says; "I started a registry for 'Sorraia-type mustangs'. It is important to make that distinction. To call those horses simply 'Sorraias' would alienate the Portuguese. Still, I believe in the importance of those horses and that they could become a valuable source at some time. If one had started a programme with selected animals back when I started this, one would already have animals by now that would make the Portuguese people's eyes bug out... Unfortunately, most Americans that got interested at one time or another never determinedly pursued this. Therefore, I have registered maybe 50 horses that are close-enough phenotypes, and a 100 more that lack a bit in one way or another (Foundation), and approximately a hundred more that show some or many of the characteristics, but lack considerably more (Tentative). Of the good types, only few made it into the Permanent division because they don't have white markings (white markings being the main reason for Sorraia types not making Permanent). There are currently 17 horses in the Permanent book, and a few more that will qualify, but have not yet been registered.

"Right now we have a situation where we find many mustangs with Sorraia characteristics, but only a few that totally look like a Sorraia. While it's obvious that we are dealing with horses that have the potential and that deserve recognition and preservation, we must not ignore that they are 'contaminated'. Only through a determined breeding effort can we hope to arrive at a population of Sorraia Mustangs that breed true, and as a whole resemble the Portuguese Sorraia in phenotype. The goal is to preserve the

Sorraia genes, not to deny their mustang background, or deliberately cover their origin and try 'selling' them as being the same as Portuguese Sorraias."

Some huge steps forward were made by idealistic breeders in Ontario, Lynne Gerard and Kevin Droski, who imported a Sorraia stallion and bred him to mustang mares with Sorraia characteristics. The foals born on their preserve are literally look-alikes to Portuguese Sorraias.

Hardy Oelke says few people are interested in preserving the Sorraia as a special horse form in its homeland. He cites an example of an owner who had sold nine stallions, only keeping one for breeding that looked more like a Lusitano than a typical Sorraia. "Breeders in Portugal are taking a renewed interest in the breeding of Sorraias – however, at least partly for the wrong reasons. The d'Andrade family preserve them in memory of their grandfather, but employing different methods than he did and mostly breeding the Sorraia like a domestic breed, not like the native wild horse their grandfather tried to re-establish and preserve. This is even more so the case with the National Stud and other institutions formerly run by the Portuguese government; many of their Sorraias aren't even kept under natural conditions. This is going to alter the Sorraia, some of the changes can already be observed. What's more, their activities introduce the Sorraia to their general horse-loving public as just another breed, so everything is moving away from the original purpose of preservation.

"I would consider a situation more desirable where all of the animals were preserved like they were when d'Andrade discovered them, even if we had even smaller numbers, instead of the somewhat increasing numbers we have today, but already lacking some of the unique characteristics that caused d'Andrade to engage in his preservation efforts."

Although a few Sorraias are today used for herding cattle, leisure and even dressage, Hardy advocates a wilder environment for breeding groups so that original traits and behaviour are more likely to be preserved, or rehabilitated. "Refuges, or preserves, like the one I established in Portugal, are the only way to reconstitute and preserve the true Sorraia, with as little intrusion by man as possible. Ideally, there would be at least one like that for Sorraia-type mustangs in North America, and/or Sorraia-type criollos in Latin America.

"Introducing them to the public as good mounts for kids to ride, like the Portuguese do now, is likely to make them more appreciated. But, it's all for the wrong reasons. You can't save the wolf by breeding wolves that behave like dogs – you will end up with dogs that may look like wolves at a first glance, but will, in reality, be much different."

Whether or not it is truly a wild horse, Hardy believes that only by treating the Sorraia as special and using it in sensitive ways – for conservation grazing, for example – can it be preserved in its original form. "Nobody claims the Sorraia to be pure anymore," he says. "However, it's still the closest thing we have to a wild, indigenous horse of southern Iberia. If it's been 'contaminated' to a degree, I'm for d'Andrade's attitude: Let's save what's left, and try to breed out any outside blood as good as we can. Or apply what the Polish zoologist Vetulani said regarding the Tarpan: Even if the whole operation aiming at the restitution of the Sorraia ultimately fails, our responsibility to following generations does not allow us to witness passively the extinction of one of the most primitive species of horses in Europe."

Sorraias
(courtesy Hardy Oelke, www.sorraia.org)

Playing God

Konik Polskis/Tarpans
(courtesy Suffolk Wildlife Trust)

The Tarpan

Just visible above tall grasses in an open Suffolk fen, a few grey backs float like seals in a green sea. But then a head lifts, with a sooty face and light mane. It is a Tarpan, one of Europe's original wild horses, grazing in a semi-feral herd to help maintain a natural ecosystem.

Or is it?

It depends on whether or not you believe that extinct breeds can be recreated from modern descendants.

Whatever your conclusion, this little horse, also named the Konik Polski, is part of a long, complicated story involving Nazi Germany, a prehistoric ox and an extinct zebra – and some visionary, controversial people.

Before domestication of the horse, the wild Takhi, or Przewalski's Horse, *Equus ferus przewalskii*, roamed eastern Asia, while the smaller, lighter, faster-moving Tarpan, *E. caballus gmelini* Antonius, was found all across Central Europe and the steppes of the Ukraine. Another subspecies, the Forest Horse, *E. caballus silvestris*, was found throughout northern European forests and marshlands, and was the founder of the heavy horse breeds.

While the Takhi was dun, the Tarpan had a grey, or 'grullo', coat, a sooty face, black legs and a black stripe down its back. And, unlike the Takhi – and the mane of the horse depicted in Pleistocene cave paintings – its black mane was not always erect, so it is thought unlikely to have been the wild horse known to early human hunters. It could even have been a semi-feral horse, or a combination of a wild remnant and domestic breeds – opinion differs about when and where domestication of the horse took place. Some believe it happened only once, around 3500 BC, north of the Black Sea. By the time domesticated horses spread across the world, wild populations were extinct. If this was the case, then all modern breeds are descended from one wild subspecies.

However, an opposing theory posits that domestication occurred in several places at different times, and remnant populations of wild horses interbred with domestic stock. This would mean that several of today's native breeds carry the genes of their wild ancestors – which may or may not have been the same subspecies. It was this latter premise that was the basis for breeding experiments by two rival camps in the 1930s in an attempt to recreate the Tarpan.

The Tarpan was first studied scientifically in 1768 by naturalist S.C. Gmelin, who described and catalogued it from four wild specimens caught near Bobrowsk in Russia. He named it after Helmut Otto Antonius, director of the Scholbrunn Zoological Gardens, Vienna. Gmelin described the Tarpan as having a disproportionately large head with a convex profile and long ears. He also mentioned the mouse-coloured coat with black points, and the dorsal stripe.

Hunted for its flesh, its forest and wetland habitat turned into farmland, in constant conflict with farmers for grazing their crops and mating with their domestic horses, the Tarpan grew ever rarer. The last wild mare fell into a crevasse in the Ukraine in 1880 while evading capture. Luckily, a small herd had previously been established in a private zoological park belonging to Count Zemoyski near Bilgoraj, Poland. These animals were later transferred to a reserve in the great forest of Bialowieza, which stretches across Belarus and Poland.

Established as a royal hunting park in 1541 for the protection of the Wisent, or European bison, the Bialowieza reserve came under the ownership of the Russian tsars in the 19th century, and was stocked with deer, elk and other game animals, while predators such as lynx and brown bear were killed off. During the First World War, much of the forest's wildlife was decimated by the German army and then Russian poachers, and all the Wisent were killed. The herd would later be re-established from 54 animals from zoos around Europe.

The Tarpan had faced a similar fate, but had escaped. Most remaining Tarpan had been given to local farmers around 1806 and been bred with domestic stock. The last captive true Tarpan died in the Munich Zoo in 1887.

The Tarpan may have become extinct, but its genes lived on. The name Konik means 'little horse' in Polish and refers to several breeds that were crossed with the Tarpans in the 18th century. However, it is generally used to describe the Bilgoraj Koniks that lived in the marshy lowlands east of the River San in eastern Poland, and has the ancestral grullo coat and dorsal stripe. Another other ancient breed believed to contain Tarpan genes is Britain's Exmoor Pony, which still lives semi-wild in southwest England, but it was the Bilgoraj Koniks that became the foundation of the new Tarpan.

In 1933, a foal was born at the Munich Zoo that looked just like its ancient ancestors, with a grullo coat and dorsal stripe. And for the director of that zoo, a grand idea began to take shape.

Zoologist Prof. Lutz Heck and his brother, Heinz, were fascinated with ancient breeds. Lutz, director of Berlin Zoo, and Heinz, director of Munich Zoo, were well-educated and knowledgeable about Germany's folklore and literature, as well as its wildlife, both living and extinct. Familiar with the current knowledge of genetics, they believed that recreating extinct breeds was simply a matter of rearranging genes by cross-breeding until the right combination was achieved. To this end, they first tried to "breed back" the extinct tur, or aurochs, the massive ox found across Europe in the early Pleistocene, by mating a Zubr (a Polish bison) with a range of European cattle breeds. They thought that by selecting for traits similar to the extinct species, they could eliminate any domestic traits and would eventually obtain an animal that exactly resembled the aurochs in behaviour, as well as in looks.

Working separately, yet with the same aims, the brothers produced hardy cattle with similar conformation. Working at the Hellabrun Zoological Gardens in Munich, Heinz crossed cattle breeds such as Angeln, Friesian, Highland, Hungarian Steppe, Podolic, Brown, Murnau-Werdenfels and Corsican; in Berlin, Lutz crossed French and Spanish fighting bulls with other breeds. Writing later in his book about the work, *Tiere – mein Abenteuer, 1952 (Animals – My Adventure)* Lutz said it was the power of the fighting bull that he most admired and wanted to reproduce in the new aurochs. His brother's animals were lost during or just after the Second World War, and all the Heck cattle existing today are descended from those bred at Hellabrun.

Also known as Reconstructed Aurochsen, *Bos primigenius taurus*, Heck cattle were originally slightly smaller than their primitive role model – an aurochs bull was said to weigh more than a ton – so African Watusi were added to the genetic mix. However, the cows became infertile, probably due to genetic drift (random changes in gene frequency) that had separated these breeds of cattle over thousands of years and made them incompatible with each other. The problem was eventually resolved by more cross-breeding.

Heck cattle still roam Europe's grasslands today, grazing nature reserves in Germany, Bavaria and France, but whether or not they are new aurochsen is fiercely debated. While some claim that Heck cattle fulfil the rôle of the aurochs in low-intensity grazing systems, others say that breeding back is not possible, and no one knows what the natural habitat of the aurochs was, anyway. Was it open parkland or forests and marshes? Some even claim that the promotion of Heck cattle is a way of allowing the native Wisent to become quietly extinct without anyone having to bother saving it.

Whether you can really call a Heck bull an aurochs is something that will never be resolved. But while no one denies that the Heck brothers produced a hardy, useful beast, their work has always been tainted — because of their association with the Third Reich.

They were said to be great friends with Herman Goering, who was delighted with their attempts to reproduce magnificent beasts from German mythology — if only so they could be hunted — and funded their work with enthusiasm. Indeed, their family had been supporters of the Nazi Party from its inception, with Lutz Heck rising to a position of prominence in Hitler's circle — close enough to exchange New Year's greetings in 1939, with hopes that "German arms" would be victorious in the coming year. By the time of the Second World War, he was in charge of all hunting and animal preserves across Germany and its occupied territories.

Lutz visited Poland in 1939 to obtain Zubr and other animals, such as Koniks, from Bialowieza Forest and the Warsaw Zoo for his breeding experiments. Some claim today that he stole them and refused to give them back after the war; but he described Poland as being under a "German administration", so he had every right to take them.

Regardless of the origins of the animals used, however, many zoologists scoffed at the Hecks' breeding programmes, saying that the Heck aurochs was just a "new cow", not a resurrection of an extinct species.

As an illustration that not everyone thought that the Hecks were off their trolleys, consider the story of another long-extinct animal that they considered recreating — the Quagga.

Equus quagga quagga was a South African zebra that used to roam the dry plains of the Karoo, north of Cape Town, South Africa, in vast herds. There were so many that 19th-century European settlers and tourists happily blasted away at them indiscriminately. Huge numbers of wild animals of all kinds were killed and their skins exported for leather goods. It's likely that the low numbers of some species today is the direct result of the decimation of the wild herds in the 19th century.

Then people started noticing that there didn't seem to be as many Quagga around as before – and it had only been described and named in 1788. Part of the problem was that every time a zebra skin taken to Europe looked slightly different to known species, it was given its own name, even if it was in reality only a colour variation of a catalogued species.

By the time the mare at the Artis Magistra Zoo in Amsterdam died in 1883, the Quagga (pronounced "quach-ha" like its call) had probably been extinct for at least two years – and no one had noticed.

Reinhold Rau was born near Frankfurt, Germany, in 1932. An enthusiastic naturalist, he grew up to be a taxidermist and worked at the South Africa Museum in Cape Town. In 1969 he found a badly mounted Quagga foal in the museum's storerooms and decided to try and restore it for display. The foal had been reared by a farmer in the 1800s after its mother had been killed by hunters, but it had only survived for a week. A local man had skinned it and sent the skin and skeleton to the museum because he'd noticed that the Quagga was becoming rarer.

The skin had not been tanned properly and still had traces of flesh adhering to it. Rau remembered the Hecks' grand rebreeding projects in Germany when he was a boy and, ignoring scientists who scoffed at his notions, preserved some of the flesh in the hope that it could be used to recreate the Quagga at a later date. No doubt he was also aware of Lutz Heck's 1955 book, *Grosswild im Etoshaland*, in which he suggested that individual Plains Zebras could be carefully selected and cross-bred to recreate the extinct Quagga, which was probably just a subspecies. This would mean that it could produce fertile offspring from mating with other subspecies of Plains Zebra.

In 1971, Rau studied all 23 mounted Quaggas in European museums (the Grant Museum at University College London has a skeleton), and gradually began to suspect that the animal was not, in fact, a separate species, but was a subspecies of the Plains Zebra, also known as Burchell's Zebra. This zebra ranges from East Africa to South Africa and has a tremendous amount of variation in its striping and colouration. The Quagga only had stripes on its oversized head, its neck and chest, with an underlying light brown colour, rather than white. Its belly and legs had no stripes – though whether this was because it lived outside the Tsetse fly area and could afford to lose the stripes that protect zebras elsewhere, or for some other reason, no one knows. In fact, before the benefit of genetic fingerprinting, some experts believed the Quagga was more closely related to the horse than to other zebras – particularly since it appeared to have the striped head of a zebra and the unstriped hind end of a horse.

Anyway, Rau took apart and remounted four of the preserved Quaggas and realised that some looked just like subspecies of the Plains Zebra that were still living. He began promoting the idea of cross-breeding zebras with Quagga-like characteristics in order to 'recreate' the extinct animal, much as the Hecks had done with the aurochs. But, like the Hecks, he was ridiculed by scientists and possible funders alike. It was to take 12 years before Rau's dream got off the ground.

In 1985, he was contacted by a retired vet, Dr J. F. Warning, who had been a friend of Lutz Heck and had accompanied him to Namibia when the German professor had written his 1955 book. Warning was an expert on animal husbandry and cattle breeding, and was to provide much-needed support to Rau during the early stages of his Quagga project.

Shortly afterwards came the big breakthrough, confirming what he and Heck had believed all along. Californian researchers, using the tissue samples that Rau had collected from the first Quagga foal he had mounted, had managed to extract mitochondrial DNA, the genetic material that is passed unaltered down the female line. Analysis showed that this material was exactly the same as that of other Plains Zebras: the Quagga had been a subspecies, not a separate species. Therefore, it could theoretically be recreated from genes in living populations.

With the financial support of several influential people, the first nine Plains Zebras were captured in March 1987 in Etosha National Park and transferred to a special breeding reserve near Robertson, in the South African Cape. The first foal was born the following year. The Quagga rebreeding project had begun.

Reinhold Rau died in February 2006, but his life's work is still going strong today. Before he died, he answered criticism that the animals being born today are not the extinct Quagga but simply lookalikes. He emphasized that the Quagga's habitat and influences were likely to have been the same as for present-day zebras, and nothing is known about any special adaptations it may have had to make it unique.

"The Quagga is a Quagga because of the way it looked," he said. "And if you produce animals that look that way, then they are Quaggas."

So was a Tarpan a Tarpan simply because of the way it looked? Along with the aurochs, the Heck brothers decided to try and breed back Europe's first horse. They had Koniks acquired from the Bialowieza Forest, and they bred the mouse-coloured ones first with Takhis then, as the Asian crosses were too heavy, with lighter ancient breeds such as Icelandic ponies, Swedish Gotlands and Norwegian Fjords.

But the Hecks had a rival. Professor Tadeusz Vetulani of Poznan University, Poland, had begun selecting Koniks and cross-breeding them towards the same goal in 1936. With the help of the Polish government, all Koniks that resembled the extinct Tarpan had been confiscated and moved to a reserve in the Bialowieza Forest – where Lutz Heck was to find them in 1939. Vetulani later established another breeding herd in the Popielno Forest. Two of his horses turned white in winter – except for a dark face, mane, tail and fetlocks – which seemed to indicate that the animals had retained some of their wild characteristics.

In the 1950s, six recreated Heck Tarpans were exported to the US from the German population to begin a new herd there. Americans are even now selectively breeding Tarpan lookalikes from the original Heck horses, and from mustangs running wild on the Western plains. But even though the American Tarpan Studbook Association states that the Tarpan can't be bred from mustangs, which are descended from horses imported by the Spanish Conquistadors, because they are too far removed from ancestral stock, the breeders don't care. Like Reinhold Rau, breeders Lenette and Gordon Stroebel of Oregon say it's the looks that matter, since there is no genetic material for cloning. "It all comes down to who can create the best lookalike," says Lenette.

Descendants of some of the Popielno Forest Tarpans are now living in Britain on the RSPB's Minsmere Nature Reserve in Suffolk, and at the Suffolk Wildlife Trust's Lopham and Redgrave Fen, along with other reserves across Europe. They are said to be ideal for grazing sensitive sites without intensive management – just as the reconstructed aurochs is considered by the Worldwide Fund for Nature to be the best substitute to fill the ecological niche of its ancestor in sites such as Lake Pape wetland reserve, Latvia.

The recreated Tarpan is strong, hardy and long-lived. It is used for showjumping, herding cattle and endurance riding. It doesn't need shoeing due to its hard, durable hooves, which also enable it to stand on marshy ground for long periods. It can survive on a range of rough grasses so can be turned out to fend for itself without much interference, and its calm temperament means it can be easily handled and poses no danger to visitors to the reserves.

But whether you call it a Tarpan or a Konik is up to you.

Konik Polskis/Tarpans
(courtesy Suffolk Wildlife Trust)

Consequences

Like with that other faithful people's companion, the dog, the human race wasn't content with letting natural selection go its own merry way to produce horses suited to a particular environment, as it had done for millions of years. Oh no: humans are working to a much quicker clock. We wanted different horses for different things, and saw no reason why they couldn't be bred and grown and shaped like greenhouse roses for a flower show.

But, like with the dog, nature hasn't always agreed with our choices, frustrating some attempts at selective breeding with unexpected side-effects. But because humans have, to a certain extent, eliminated natural selection, animals that would not have survived in the wild because of genetic abnormalities are allowed to live and pass on undesirable traits that would otherwise have disappeared. This is not a problem in the case of say, a light coat colour, which may not have provided good enough camouflage for a wild mare to survive so she could pass on those genes to her offspring; today's horses don't have to worry about predators, so coat colour is not an issue.

But when that trait is linked with a gene for a disorder that may result in death, it's another matter.

Fortunately, the horse has a relatively low incidence of inherited disorders compared to the dog and other domesticated species (although a search on Online Mendelian Inheritance in Animals, OMIA, maintained by the Australian National Genomic Information Service, produced 188 results). As well as physical deformities, genetic mutations can cause congenital (before-birth) abnormalities, such as heart defects or inverted eyelids, as well as disorders or syndromes. In the latter case, these are often more likely to affect certain breeds than others.

Genes for each trait are carried in every individual (whether horse or human) as two copies, or alleles, one copy from each parent. Each allele can be dominant or recessive, the dominant version masking the effects of the recessive allele. Only if both parents contribute recessive alleles will the trait for that gene be expressed in the foal. And if that allele has a mutation associated with a disorder, that's bad news for the poor foal.

A mutated copy of the gene inherited with a normal one is said to be in the heterozygous state (think heterosexual – one of each), while two mutated alleles inherited together are said to be homozygous (think homosexual – two of a kind). It is this state that tends to result in a disorder being expressed, whereas a horse that is heterozygous for the trait (one normal, one mutant) will usually just pass it on to its offspring (an exception being ASD, which can develop from both a heterozygous and homozygous inheritance – the foal only has to inherit one copy of the gene from one parent . An 'autosomal gene' is carried on a chromosome other than a sex chromosome (the female X or male Y), which means that either sex is affected equally by a disorder caused by that gene.

Certain breeds seem more susceptible to genetic disorders than others – Arabians and draught horses, for example, particularly American Belgians, which were heavily inbred once imports of the breed from Europe to the US ended in 1940. Other disorders can be traced directly back to a single individual – such as the champion Quarter Horse Poco Bueno, many of whose descendants carry the mutation that causes HC, or HERDA. Yet whereas in the wild, that mutation would have eventually disappeared as all individuals in which it was expressed died, today, thanks to selective breeding many humans are still playing Russian roulette with horses whose genetic inheritance causes great suffering and could even prove to be their death.

Many of these genes can now be identified so that further breeding is prevented, but in some cases either there is no current test for the disorder, or the lineage is unknown – or, in at least one outrageous case, breeders are willing to risk their horse's health because the mutation 'improves' the animal's bearing for showing.

Not all foals that inherit a gene for a disorder can pass it on: in some cases, the foal, having two copies of a particular allele, develops the disorder itself and cannot survive. This is the case with Severe Combined Immunodeficiency (SCID or just CID). Around 3 per cent of Arabian foals are born with this disorder, but they die within their first few months because the condition disables their immune system and their bodies can't fight infection. The carriers, either the stallion or the mare, look perfectly healthy, but since the disorder is inherited as an autosomal recessive allele, if two carriers are mated together, the resulting foal has two copies of the recessive mutated gene, so has SCID.

The disorder was first reported in Australia in the 1960s, and in the US in 1973. Although there was initially denial among breeders of Arabians that such an ancient, pure-blooded breed could be subject to genetic deformities, it has now been accepted that the older a breed – and the more time available for human-controlled matings – the more likely that genetic mutations will arise and be passed on to the next generation, and the more incidences of a disorder will appear.

There is now a DNA test that allows breeders to avoid mating two carriers of SCID together, and a count of white blood cells in a foal will establish whether it probably carries the disease. A count of less than 1,000 white cells per mm^3, and a lack of immunoglobulin M are diagnostic of SCID – a healthy foal should have a white blood cell count of between 2,500 and 3,000 per mm^3. A suspected SCID foal will also have an underdeveloped thymus and lymph nodes, which can be confirmed by post mortem.

Another disorder that is fatal for a foal inheriting both alleles for it is Glycogen branching enzyme deficiency (GBED). This has only relatively recently been identified in horses – so far, only Quarter Horses and Paint horses – but has been known in humans for some time. The mutation causes the lack of a working enzyme needed to store sugar molecules as glycogen, which means that tissues that use glycogen as an energy source – brain, heart muscle and skeletal tissue – cannot function properly. Foals with this disorders are stillborn or die after a few months from heart failure or seizures due to low blood sugar, or are aborted and resorbed by the mare. Symptoms (there are many, which is why it has taken so long to be identified as a single disorder) include a low temperature, weakness, a high respiratory rate, contracted tendons and an inability to get up from lying on its side. Afflicted foals also often have a low white blood cell count.

Like the human form, equine GBED is inherited as an autosomal (non-sex-linked) recessive gene carried by either a male or a female, both of which are affected equally. A foal with two copies of the recessive gene will have the disorder. However, there is a DNA test available to determine whether a stallion or mare is a carrier before breeding.

Lavender Foal Syndrome, or Dilute White, found in Egyptian and part-Egyptian Arabians, causes severe neurological problems. The foal is larger than normal, can't stand or nurse, has rapid eye movements and joint rigidity. The name of the disorder stems from the colour of its coat, which is often a light lavender or pink, due either to abnormal clumping of pigment in the hair or cyanosis (lack of oxygen) during birth. The afflicted foal usually dies within 48 hours of birth.

Overo Lethal White Syndrome (OLWS, Lethal White) is an example of a fatal genetic disorder linked to coat colour. Also known as 'equine aganglionic megacolon', this disorder is found in some Paint Horses with white markings in an 'overo' pattern, particularly a 'frame overo'. (There are two types of Paint patterning, overo and tobiano. The tobiano has white legs, a dark head and white spots arranged vertically, and does not seem to be affected by the defective gene).

There are three types of overo, a Spanish term for egg-like. In a 'frame overo', the horse has dark legs, sometimes with white socks, and white spots on the head and horizontally on the sides and neck. These horses often have one or two blue eyes. 'Sabino', or 'calico overo', horses have white on the legs, head and belly. These also often have blue eyes. The third type of overo is the much rarer 'splashed white', with a lot of white on the head, and white spots on the legs, belly and sides. Again, they may have blue eyes.

The OLWS mutation causes a fault in the proliferation and/or migration of nerve stem cells in the developing embryo, so that the foal is born with a lack of nerve cells to the last part of the large intestine. This means that the all-white foal cannot pass faeces. Although it will suckle normally when first born, as soon as the intestinal tract is full up, it will stop eating and either die or have to be put down. Although the gene for the overo coat colour is dominant, the OLWS gene is believed to be recessive and lethal only in its homozygous state – that is, when a foal has inherited two mutated copies of the gene from both its mother and its father. When two overo horses are mated – or those with overos in their lineage – 25 per cent of their offspring will be all-white and may have Overo Lethal White Syndrome (provided there is a carrier in its parentage).

The syndrome has also been reported in Pintos, Miniature Horses and Thoroughbreds with a Paint Horse in their lineage, and because of the upsurge in popularity in the US of the so-called Gypsy Horse, the condition is being reported more frequently. A DNA test is now available to prevent the mating of two carriers.

Other genetic disorders linked to coat colour include an autosomal gene for a roan coat in Belgians that is lethal when two alleles are inherited by a foal, and the nasty (but not fatal) Anterior Segment Dysgenesis (ASD), found mostly in horses with chocolate or flaxen coats and a white mane and tail.

Predominantly thought of as being a problem only in the Rocky Mountain Saddle Horse in the US, ASD has also recently been found in other breeds carrying the silver dapple gene – including the Shetland Pony, Miniature Horse, Kentucky Mountain Saddle Horse, Morgan, American Bashkir-Curly, Mountain Pleasure Horse, Haflinger and Naragansett Pacer. It has been studied extensively in the Rocky Mountain Saddle Horse, however, and that breed's association first described it.

The disorder is due to a gene inherited in a co-dominant manner – that is, in two forms, or phenotypes, and the unlucky foal that inherits even one copy of the gene can suffer problems with the front (anterior) part of its eyes. Horses that inherit only one ASD allele (heterozygous) may develop cysts in the eye, while those inheriting two copies of the gene (homozygous) may develop complex lesions and abnormalities of the eye. In the heterozygous state, the gene causes fluid-filled cysts arising from the ciliary body – a structure behind the iris – and the retina. The horse may also have an abnormally shaped retina. The gene inherited in the homozygous state gives rise to multiple anomalies in the eye – including cysts, bulging eyeballs (megalocornea), very small eyes (microphthalmia), abnormally shaped pupil (dyscoria), a clouded lens (nuclear cataract), iris abnormalities, partial displacement of the lens (subluxation), and small pupils that don't dilate.

Astonishingly, this condition is not considered a serious health threat. In the majority of cases, the anomalies do not seem to impair vision, and the disorder is not fatal. Researchers are developing DNA markers in the search for the gene responsible.

There are numerous physical abnormalities that can be inherited, and often these, too, seem to afflict certain breeds more than others. For example, patellar luxation tends to affect Shetland Ponies and Miniature Horses. The patella (kneecap) is displaced or migrates to the outside of the knee. Signs include the newborn foal crouching, unable to extend its legs fully.

Hereditary junctional mechanobullous is sometimes found in Belgian foals. The basement membrane of the foot separates and sloughs off the hooves by the age of 12 days.

Another congenital affliction of American Belgians and Saddlebreds in the US, and other draught breeds in Europe, is Junctional epidermolysis bullosa (JEB). This is caused by a recessive gene, so a foal would have to inherit both copies for the disorder to be expressed. JEB is a group of skin and mucous membrane diseases resulting in blisters and ulcers in response to mechanical trauma. There are three types, each characterised by a different level of skin separation and by the proteins involved. In Belgians, there is an extra cytosine – one of the amino acids that makes up protein – in the DNA sequence, and a premature stop codon that ends the sequence before a particular instruction is expressed properly. This prevents the formation of a necessary protein, and results in skin lesions and hair, loss of hooves and separation of the coronary band.

JEB was first recorded in Sweden in 1934, and the reason that this disorder become prevalent in the US is believed to be because imports of Belgians ended in the 1940s during the Second World War, and all new animals of that breed were produced from the US population, many of whom were related to each other. JEB has also been recorded in two French draught breeds: Breton and Comtois. Carriers can be identified by a test on the mane and tail hair.

In some cases, a disorder can be traced back through a particular line. All incidence of Hereditary Equine Regional Dermal Asthenia (HERDA), for example, known to some vets as Hyperelastosis Cutis (HC), can be traced back to champion Quarter Horse Poco Bueno, born in 1944, and his line. He and his sire, King, were legends in their time, winning many shows and siring many champion performance, cutting and showing horses. HERDA was first recognized as a disorder in 1971, but more incidences are cropping up all the time as related horses are mated. The mutation causes a defect in the collagen that keeps skin layers together – under a saddle or other skin trauma the outer skin layer separates and splits, leaving scars. New damage occurs regularly, and the skin is also highly susceptible to sunburn.

Another affliction of some Shetlands and draught Suffolk Punches is Narcolepsy, sometimes known as the Fainting Disease. Not much is known about it, but it is believed to be inherited down particular lines of some breeds, including Welsh ponies, Miniature Horses, Thoroughbreds, Quarter Horses, Morgans, Appaloosas, and Standardbreds.

Other physical disorders to affect certain breeds, or age classes, include Inguinal Hernia, often found in Standardbred and draught breeds, which is manifested in a large scrotal sac; Degenerative Joint Disease, which afflicts Icelandic Horses; and Cushing's Disease, which is most common in Morgans, as well as ponies, and in horses over 20 years old. It is caused by a benign tumour in the pituitary gland that stimulates the gland into producing more hormone than necessary. One result is usually a long, luxuriant coat that is not moulted in the summer. The condition also causes an imbalance in the adrenal gland, as well as laminitis, foot abscesses, loss of muscle along the rump and topline, and excessive drinking and urination. Horses with Cushing's can be treated with drugs, their health improving enough to prolong their lives by another five years or more.

Other inherited defects include parrot mouth, holes in the heart and dwarfism. Many other disorders and illnesses are thought to be inherited, but there is often not enough research to prove it one way or another. Examples of suspected inherited disorders include Sweet Itch, a skin allergy to midge bites, particularly found in Icelandic Horses, and Recurrent Exertional Rhabdomyolysis Syndrome (a form of azoturia, or tying-up). This latter is often found in young female Thoroughbreds and Standardbreds, and is seen as painful muscle spasms, profuse sweating and difficulty in breathing after exercise. Research has shown that a predisposition to get this particular form of the syndrome (there are several, with many causes), could be inherited as a dominant gene, meaning that 50 per cent of foals would be likely to inherit the gene from a carrier parent. Whether or not they develop the disorder may depend on training, nutrition and management.

Despite the generally high level of awareness of inherited disorders, not to mention the battery of tests available, a few unscrupulous breeders continue to think of their bank accounts, rather than the welfare of their horses. Hyperkalemic periodic paralysis (HYPP) is a case in point. It should have been eradicated years ago, but because of perceived 'benefits' to show horses with the disorder, some owners are continuing to breed on carriers, even knowing of the suffering that could be inflicted on the next generation of horses.

The disorder affects large number of Quarter Horses, Appaloosas and Paint Horses descended from the stallion Impressive. The mutation is a dominant trait, so only one parent need be a carrier for the allele to be passed on to the foal, but 25 per cent of foals from a carrier will inherit both copies of the gene and have HYPP. Affected horses have muscle tremors and become temporarily paralysed. Severe attacks can result in respiratory and heart failure and death. Horses with two copies of the gene do not survive very long, but those with only one allele can live relatively normal lives if their diet is controlled. A DNA test is available for breeders.

The American Quarter Horse (QH) stallion Impressive was one of the top QH stallions of all time, winning 31 blue ribbons in the show ring at halter out of 31 attempts. He produced a long line of champion foals – out of the top 15 halter champions of 1993, 13 were descendants of Impressive. In 1993, it was estimated that 55,000 Quarter Horses, Paints and Appaloosas worldwide were descended from him. As a consequence, the disorder is also known as Impressive Syndrome.

The mutation causes a defect in a protein called the voltage-gaited sodium channel, a tiny opening in the membranes of muscle cells that controls the movement of sodium particles in and out of the cell. Sodium particles carry a charge that changes the voltage current of the muscle cell, allowing it to contract or relax. Potassium leaks from inside the muscle cells into the bloodstream, raising the concentration of potassium in the blood. This overloads the system with potassium and causes attacks of involuntary muscle twitching, skin tremors, paralysis of the hindquarters and excessive yawning. In extreme cases, paralysis of the muscles around the heart and lungs results in death from heart attack or suffocation. Not all victims show outward signs of the disease, and many can live without suffering the worst effects of it.

Symptoms of HYPP often resemble those of tying-up syndrome, but horses with HYPP seem normal after an attack of muscle tremors ends. Tying-up syndrome sufferers have a stiff gait and firm, painful muscles in the hind limbs, rump and/or back. However, tremors in horses with this condition – and in others – occur in association with exercise, whereas HYPP causes muscle activity when the horse is at rest, while feeding, or immediately following some sort of stress, such as transport, a change in feeding regime, or illness. HYPP may also be mistaken for colic if the horses cannot stand but it is conscious and aware and does not seem to be in pain. Its loud breathing may sometimes be confused with choke or respiratory illness.

Treatment over the long term involves regular exercise and access to a large pasture. feeding should be regular, and the diet should be managed to avoid a high potassium intake – for example, feeding oats, corn or barley, all of which are low in potassium.

Another consequence of human-controlled breeding of horses, although not strictly a disorder, is an inherited condition of grey Thoroughbreds. All Thoroughbreds in the UK are descended from a small group of horses brought over from the Middle East in the 1700s, including three Arabians – the Godolphin Arabian, the Byerly Turk and the Darley Arabian. The gene for a grey coat is believed to have been introduced into the new Thoroughbred line by a stallion called Alcock's Arabian in 1720. Grey coats are still extremely rare in Thoroughbreds – only about 3 per cent have that coat colour. They are usually born black, chestnut or bay, then develop the dappled coat later in life. Sadly, the grey gene comes with a price. Like the silver dapple gene that causes ASD cysts in the Rocky Mountain Saddle Horse, among other breeds, the grey gene in Thoroughbreds leads to skin tumours, or melanomas, once the horse reaches 10 years of age.

The problem is particularly noticeable in UK racehorses because their breeding has been so tightly controlled over the years, and they are all descended from the original horses imported to begin the Thoroughbred line in the 18th century. According to Dr Matthew Binns of the Animal Health Trust in Suffolk, which is working on the Horse Genome Project, all the grey horses on the racecourse have a piece of DNA that comes from the original founder. Ironically, it is also because of that tightly controlled breeding and registration of Thoroughbreds over the centuries that breeders can see any abnormalities or conditions that crop up regularly, and researchers thus have a better chance of identifying the genes responsible and advising on future breeding.

Although it seems that many inherited disorders appear to affect the Quarter Horse, this may simply be a case of better reporting than for other breeds. According to Quarter Horse breeder Anna Burns, who is on the council of the American Quarter Horse Association-UK (AQHA-UK), nearly all cases of HERDA and other disorders have been found in the US, simply because there are a lot of breeders there. "You have to remember that the Quarter Horse is probably the biggest horse registry in the world, so they are bound to throw up more of these rather unusual conditions, which, of course, do not only affect Quarter Horses" she says.

"I have never had anything suffering from these conditions and most of the conditions are, in fact, very rare in Quarter Horses apart from, perhaps, HYPP, which only affects stock tracing to one Thoroughbred-line halter-bred stallion, Impressive. The AQHA has recently made a rule which will shortly phase out registration of any animal which tests positive for this. Unfortunately, horses have continued to be bred from HYPP-positive lines in the US because they are extremely successful show lines, so there has been little voluntary control there. I think it was a case of money talks and, of course, the Quarter Horse industry is multi-million-dollar over there. The blood test result has had, for some time, to be shown on the registration certificate. I do know of a handful of horses that have been affected in this country but they are no longer with us.

"As to the other nasty conditions, I have never heard of any horses in this country being affected. This is not to say that they never have been, though the conditions do seem to be fairly new. It is a pretty close-knit association, and people tend to know each other, so I think one would hear, even if it was kept quiet (which I think it possibly has been in the States to some extent). I should add, however, that I have not personally come across any horses in the States that have been afflicted, either. Americans tend to leave these things to one's own conscience. There is no stallion licensing scheme in the States, or here. We used to have a scheme some years ago, but we felt we had to go the way of the States (to some people's annoyance). If your horse is parrot-mouthed or chryptorchid it should be mentioned on your registration form but, apart from that it is up to the individual."

Dr Caroline Hahn of the Royal (Dick) School of Veterinary Studies, University of Edinburgh, agrees that most inherited disorders are likely to be seen in the US, rather than the UK, if only because of the larger population of each breed. "We haven't seen any [disorders] at the University of Edinburgh in the last 15 years, but our population of Quarter Horses is tiny."

Even though breed associations are banning registry of carriers of some disorders, the conditions would be "unlikely to be eliminated, but it would probably help," she adds. "HYPP in Europe is unlikely to be seen now that heterozygotes can't be registered as breeding stock."

However, despite the tests available and the knowledge about the disorders, some unscrupulous breeders are unlikely to change their ways simply because their horse is shown to be a carrier.

"I doubt it would do much if that line of animal is winning shows," she says.

And although unravelling the horse's genome will contribute to the possible diagnosis of genetic disorders, "treatment and predictability are likely to be a long way off."

As far as Overo Lethal White Syndrome goes, again, this is relatively rare in the UK, "due to the American Paint Horse only really becoming popular here in the last seven or eight years," according to Sue Painter, president of the UK Paint Horse Association (UKPHA). "We have had some experience of it since, and we are trying to educate people now about these genetic disorders," she says. "We strongly encourage people to do their homework before breeding, not only frame overo to frame overo, but any coloured/Paint breeding, as the overo gene is recessive and can appear without warning even from solid [colour] matings (although less likely) and from tovero (tobiano/overo) matings. We strongly suggest that only a OLWS N/N stallion (with dominant genes) is used and encourage that overos are tested for the gene, too."

While disorders may be rare in some regions of the world and prevalent in others, the fact remains that natural selection would have weeded out the weak generations ago, if it were not for human intervention.

But humans have gone even further, as we shall see in the next chapter.

© Lynn Parr

Handmade Horses

So you've bred the perfect horse. It has everything you want: looks, speed, character, pedigree. But when you try to pass on those traits, there's no guarantee that its offspring will be exactly the same – in fact, thanks to the fact that sexual reproduction is based on inherited genes from two parents, it's quite likely that the foals will not be identical to your ideal horse. And if the horse is a gelding, there's no chance of reproducing it, anyway.

And what about extinct breeds – how can they be brought back?

So what if you could build a horse from scratch, bypassing nature altogether, thus preventing the chance that unwanted traits will be inherited – as nature has done with parthenogenesis in insects and vegetative reproduction in plants? If your horse was a champion, you could make a fortune from selling identical copies of it, since the buyers would be virtually guaranteed a champion of their own – wouldn't they? And endangered breeds could be saved or even brought back from extinction.

In 2003, some scientists did just that, creating the world's first clone of a horse. But was it a dream come true?

What exactly is a clone? Basically, a clone is an individual that is genetically identical to another. Normal reproduction can sometimes produce clones in the form of identical twins, when a fertilised embryo, or 'zygote', splits into two, which each develop into a separate individual. Clones can, however, be created artificially.

In Artificial Embryo Twinning, an embryo is literally divided in a petri dish – like the natural formation of identical twins – then the individual cells are implanted in a surrogate mother (or mothers). In Somatic Cell Nuclear Transfer (SCNT), the DNA in the egg of one animal is replaced by the DNA of the animal to be cloned. It was this method that was used to clone Dolly the sheep, and is currently used to clone horses.

Firstly, the nucleus (which contains the DNA on the chromosomes) is removed from an egg cell, and replaced with the nucleus from a 'somatic' cell, a cell from any part of a body except egg or sperm. Then the egg cell and its new DNA are fused together using an electrical pulse and treated in a chemical medium that kick-starts its development into an embryo, which can be brought to term in a surrogate mother. Thus, Dolly the sheep was created when a somatic cell nucleus from an adult sheep's udder was transferred into the egg of another sheep. It didn't matter that the new DNA came from an adult sheep's udder; it was 'reprogrammed' in the egg cell to develop into an embryo.

To put it more simply: in normal sexual reproduction, a fertilised egg, or zygote, has two sets of chromosomes – one from the mother and one from the father. Thus the traits of both parents are inherited by the offspring. In SCNT, however, a single set of chromosomes from an unfertilised egg cell is removed. The somatic cell nucleus that is put into the 'empty' egg already has two sets of chromosomes from the animal to be cloned. Therefore, in the resulting offspring, both sets of chromosomes come from one 'parent' and inherit all its traits.

The world's first horse, Prometea, was cloned in Italy in 2003 – though she wasn't the first equine clone. That honour went to Idaho Gem, a mule born in Idaho, US, also in 2003. Prometea was cloned from skin cells from a Halflinger mare – who also happened to be her surrogate mother, although the Italian researchers had implanted the manipulated eggs into several other mares, as well. This means that Prometea made history not only as the world's first cloned horse, but also as the first clone to be born to her own genetic twin.

Since then, other horse and mule clones have been born, including five colts to champion cutting horse Smart Little Lena (cutting is separating cattle from a herd) and a foal to top showjumper ET. All the clones were to be used for breeding, rather than to become competitors in their own right. Interestingly, although ET and his clone have an identical genetic makeup, they have different facial markings. And despite these identical genes, there is actually no guarantee that clones of champions will automatically be champions themselves – there are too many other variables, such as training, environment, general health and so on.

All equine clones so far have been produced in the US or continental Europe. In the UK, the government has given the go-ahead for horse cloning for research, but banned the cloning of sport horses for commercial purposes. Racehorse clones are also banned by international rules – though the first mule clones are already competing in races in the US (their cloning was financially backed by a mule-racing enthusiast), and there are no restrictions on clones competing in events such as dressage and showjumping (because of the amount of training involved). So, theoretically, now even a champion gelding can pass on his genetic material to a new generation. As Prof. William 'Twink' Allen, of the Equine Fertility Unit in Newmarket, says, cloning "won't recreate a champion horse, because other factors intervene, but it can reproduce its testicles." So now you can have a clone of your champion eventer created from just a few skin cells – and around $150,000.

So what's the catch? Why has the UK government banned cloning when it can clearly overcome the uncertainties of ordinary breeding? Even though the horse has far fewer problems in producing clones than sheep and cattle, the success rate is still very low – the Idaho team recorded a 2.7 per cent foaling rate in 2003, while in 2005, a Texas A&M University team reported a horse cloning success rate of only 0.7 per cent. In other words, for 28 mule clone embryos implanted, 25 'failed' (died) within the first 80 days. The first horse clone, Prometea, was the only successful foal out of four pregnancies from 328 implanted embryos. In most species, cloned embryos fail to develop normally, or the foetus is stillborn or has birth defects.

The high failure rate in cloning could be because the adult genes transplanted into the carrier egg are not properly reprogrammed, and so affect the embryo. Researchers in Cambridge have another theory. They discovered that there is often damage to the cell signalling mechanism: the signals within an embryo that tell its cells how to develop were abnormal. This may also mean that an apparently healthy clone will develop health problems later in life.

According to Prof. Wolf Reik, head of the team at the Babraham Institute, "What could happen is that the clone is born looking quite normal and its early life is quite normal, but later on these animals could develop all sorts of diseases."

Horses don't seem to have as many problems in cloning as other livestock, such as sheep and cattle. Prof. Gordon Woods of the University of Idaho, part of the team that cloned the first mules, thinks this may be partly due to technical differences in the methods used. "For example, we minimized in vitro handling and incubation of the oocytes [eggs] and cloned embryos in our system compared to what is generally done during ruminant cloning. Besides technical differences, it is likely due to species differences, such as the different type of placental development that occurs in equines compared to ruminants, since many of the problems seen with ruminant clones have been due to placental abnormalities during gestation."

Equine vet Dr David McDowell does not think the UK government will change its mind about cloning any time soon. "Cloning not only involves potential suffering to the cloned offspring (abnormalities, early death, and so on), but also subjects many surrogate mares to invasive procedures, as cloned embryos are implanted into them and their hormone systems are manipulated to encourage the development and continuation of the pregnancy. Birth problems may also arise, particularly if there is a discrepancy in size between host mother and offspring.

"It is not often realised that at the current state of knowledge many, many more mares are subjected to treatment than become pregnant, and many of the resultant pregnancies become abnormal and either cause abortions or are deliberatively terminated. In one [research] paper I saw something like a hundred mares were implanted to achieve about six pregnancies with, I think, two live offspring. It is the failure rate which causes as much concern as the suffering of the successful cloned offspring. On the basis of preventing all this suffering it is a good question, why use cloning techniques at all?"

So is cloning ethical? Apart from allowing gelded animals to reproduce and perhaps saving endangered breeds, some researchers claim cloning methods can be used for the benefit of human medicine. Indeed, the purpose of creating cloned farm animals is often so they can be used to study diseases, or to produce useful proteins or antibodies in their milk or replacement organs for people.

Prof. Gordon Woods of the University of Idaho, who was part of the team that cloned the first three mules, became interested in horses because stallions don't develop prostate cancer. He found that horses have much more calcium around and within their cells, and a much slower metabolism than humans. Adjusting the calcium concentration in the fluid around the cells dramatically increased the team's cloning success rate, and Prof. Woods believes that the knowledge of microbiology gained in cloning will provide important insights in treating cancer in humans.

However, such justification doesn't convince everyone. Vet Dr McDowell says: "I am often suspicious that researchers dress up their desire to investigate cloning with vague promises that it will help cure cancer, prevent mental degeneration, or other such wonders. It needs a scientific mind to read the small print to deduce the exact nature of each project and the likelihood of success."

He doesn't fully dismiss cloning if "something could be achieved that was worthwhile and could not be achieved any other way". However, "at the current state of knowledge, cloning is such a precarious technique that I have doubts as to whether it can be promoted as a useful research tool. Possibly the best work that could be done at the moment, and on a limited scale, would be to improve the technique of cloning itself, but if this is to be done with minimal suffering, then small numbers of animals need to be used and so any meaningful results would take years to produce. If fast progress has to be made, then large numbers of animals need to be involved and the potential for large-scale suffering amplifies. From a welfare perspective I see little value in cloning and a lot of potential and actual welfare problems. So I would suggest that the welfare perspective is to be against cloning, without necessarily closing the door totally in all instances."

Prof. Woods disputes that the mares suffer and says cloning techniques are improving all the time. "Mares used for cloning are managed and handled no differently than they are for other non-cloning uses. I am confident there will be continued refinement of the technology that will lead to further increases in efficiency of the process."

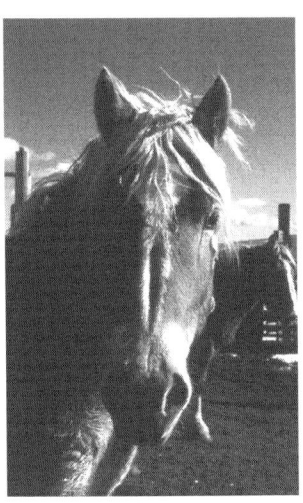

Belgians
© Lynn Parr

An Uncertain Future

Shire Horse
© Lynn Parr

On the Edge

Although so many equine breeds have been saved from extinction, many more could disappear in the next few years. But is this as gloomy a picture as it sounds? After all, it often depends on where you live.

For example, in 2009, the mighty Shire was said to be on the edge of the abyss. The media went crazy. Here was an equine link to the knights who defended the castles that define the British countryside, who actually lived the colourful, romantic history on which the country still thrives; yet it had been allowed to decline unnoticed. Network television news, magazines and newspapers featured reminiscences of the gentle giants galloping across the green fields or plodding along country lanes. "Only a handful left!" screamed the headlines. The nation's horse is dying out!

Then someone read the small print on the press release. Yes, there were only a few new Shires born in Britain that year – 150 mares, with 50 of them sold abroad, leaving a deficit in the population. But only in England. In the rest of the world, compared to other breeds the Shire was actually doing fine, particularly in North America.

That's not to say that there are some breeds in danger of dying out all across the world – the Sorraia and the Eriskay Pony, for example. But should we be concerned when a breed becomes 'extinct' in our home country, when it is flourishing elsewhere?

Geneticist Dr Dawn Teverson says yes. "Many rare breeds have genes which are peculiar to the breed and will be lost forever if that breed becomes extinct. Farming increasingly involves countryside management rather than merely crop and livestock production, and equines have an important role to play in conservation grazing situations as well as their numerous other roles. Native rare breeds are hardy and able to survive in situations where many other breeds would very quickly perish.

"As well as the heritage value of our own native breeds, it is important that the mother breed societies in the UK conserve breeds in their own environment where their breeding can be guided and regulated, for the genetic health of the breed. There is a great danger with leaving others to do the job – if it goes wrong we would have no one to blame but ourselves."

Likewise, Prof. D. Phillip Sponenberg, of the Virginia-Maryland Regional College of Veterinary Medicine, points out that breeds change over the years, either due to artificial selection by humans, or by adapting naturally to their environment and conditions, so populations should always be preserved wherever they are found. For example, the Colonial Spanish horse in North America is very different to the Iberian types from which it probably came. "Whatever the origin, it is undeniable that the resulting horse is distinct from most other horse types, which is increasingly important as most other horse breeds become homogenised around a very few types dominated by the Arabian, Thoroughbred, and Warmbloods," he says. "These three are responsible for the general worldwide erosion of genetic variability in horse breeds. The Spanish type subsequently became rare and is now itself in need of conservation. The horse currently in Spain is distinct, through centuries of divergent selection, from the Colonial Spanish Horse. The result is that the New World remnants are very important to overall conservation, since the New World varieties are closer in type to the historic horse of the Golden Age of Spain than are the current horses in Iberia."

An excellent illustration of how quickly breeds can change according to conditions and environment is seen in the wild horses of the Namib Desert. Bloodtyping shows them to be related to European breeds such as the Trakehner and Thoroughbred, and it's thought they were brought to the Namib in German colonial times – though no one is sure of the details. One story says the

German army brought in thousands of Trakehners as cavalry horses to put down tribal rebellions and to use in the First World War; another says they were brought in by Germans building a railway between Lüderitz and Keetmanshoop. Yet another legend claims the horses are the descendants of more than 300 imported to Castle Duwisib, 200km north of where they are found today in a reserve in the Namib-Naukluft Park – by Baron Hans-Heinrich von Wolf, who tried to breed a new African saddle horse. When he was killed at the Somme in 1916, the horses were left to fend for themselves. Some people, however, claim the wild horses were introduced by the Nama tribe much earlier, though DNA research has shown this to be unlikely. Despite freezing nights and temperatures of 40°C in the shade during the day, the horses cling on, relying on an underground spring dripping from a tap into a water trough at an abandoned railway station – along with alfalfa taken to them by local farmers in times of need.

But what's even more interesting than the fact of their existence in such an inhospitable place is that bloodtyping has shown them to possess a unique factor in their blood group, the benefit of which is yet to be found. They are also highly inbred and have a genetic profile not found in any other type of horse. Does this make them a new breed? Or, at least, on the way to becoming one?

Is any breed, in fact, a constant from one year to the next, or one location to another? Isn't extinction nature's way of cleaning house?

Vet Dr David McDowell says while he regrets any breeds or species becoming extinct, if they had died out naturally, bringing them back may not necessarily solve the problems that led to their extinction in the first place. On the other hand, "If [breeds] were allowed to die out due to human intervention, this was probably because they were of limited use."

Even with the help of some local residents, the Namib horses could easily be wiped out by the next severe drought, as they almost were in 1999, or by urban development. Some people would not care if this happened, as they don't regard the horses as 'natural' wild animals – just as the mustangs of the American West are reviled by ranchers as 'range maggots', no better than city pigeons. However, as geneticist Dr Dawn Teverson says, "Rare breeds of any species, but specifically equines, are not natural, so extinction could never be 'what nature intends'."

The Namib horses are not the only breeds facing extinction. The Convention on Biological Diversity, adopted at the Earth Summit in Rio de Janeiro in 1992, obligates governments to protect the diversity of their country's agricultural livestock breeds as well as of their wildlife. In compliance with this, the UK's Rare Breeds Survival Trust has a Watch List of breeds in categories from 'At Risk' to 'Critical', as well as a category called 'Traditional' for breeds with a larger population, but which still need a weather eye kept on them. The equine breeds considered 'Critical', with a UK population consisting of fewer than 300, are the Cleveland Bay, Suffolk Punch, Eriskay Pony and Dales Pony. The Exmoor Pony and the Hackney, both Horse and Pony, are 'Endangered', with fewer than 500 animals. On the 'Vulnerable' list (fewer than 900) are the Dartmoor, Fell, Highland and Welsh Mountain Section A ponies, while the Clydesdale is considered 'At Risk', with fewer than 1,500. The Shire is in the 'Traditional' category, with 3,000 or fewer animals in the UK, but with not enough mares being born each year to sustain the population over the long term.

The **Cleveland Bay** originated in the Cleveland Hills of northeast England during the Middle Ages, when the monasteries bred powerful packhorses to carry trade goods such as wool. In Yorkshire they were known as Chapman horses, the name given to peddlers. In the 17th century, many Chapman horses were bred with Barbs, particularly around the Whitby area, and heavier breeds were also introduced, producing an all-round draught animal, the Cleveland, for agriculture and transport. By the 18th century, however, roads had improved so there was a demand for carriage horses, and many Clevelands were crossed with Thoroughbreds to produce fine-boned, elegant coach horses. These were exported all over the country and were much in demand by the gentry – Queen Elizabeth II still breeds them and they are seen drawing gorgeous coaches on State occasions. As with many breeds, however, hundreds were lost during the First World War when local horses were requisitioned by the army and taken to Flanders.

The **Suffolk Punch** has the earliest stud book of any breed and is the oldest still existing in the same form. All today's Suffolks can trace their lines back to a single stallion, Crisp's Horse of Ufford, born in 1768, though the breed is believed to have existed long before that – it was described in the 15th century, and may have been around for 200 years even before then, perhaps originating in Belgium. It is sometimes called the Suffolk Punch due to its short legs and massive body, and always comes in one of seven shades of chesnut (spelled with only one 't'). During the 19th century, hundreds of Suffolks were employed on farms throughout Suffolk and Norfolk, though were not seen further afield. The breed declined with the coming of agricultural machinery, and in 1966, only nine foals were born. Local breeders came to its rescue to prevent its extinction, though it is still critically endangered around the world.

The other breed on the RBST Watch List to be classified as 'Critical' is the **Dales Pony**. Originally bred in the Pennine dales from Derbyshire to the Scottish border, the pony was used for transporting lead from the mines in the hills to ports on the northeast coast. Each pony was expected to carry two 'pigs', or hundredweight, of lead. Blended with the Scottish Galloway, the pony was strong, rugged and surefooted, and could survive in the harsh conditions of the northern uplands. As well as being used in the lead and coal mining industries, the Dales Pony was a favourite with farmers, both as a draught animal and saddle horse. In the 18th century, the pony was further improved by crossing with the Yorkshire Roadster and the Norfolk Cob, both renowned for a fast trot. Most Dales ponies alive today can trace a line back to the foundation sire of the Norfolk Cob, Shales the Original, a descendant of the Darley Arabian, who was one of the founders of the Thoroughbred. Again, however, mechanisation and war took their toll, and it's only the dedication of a handful of breeders that has kept the Dales Pony from vanishing into history.

Similar organisations to the RBST exist around the world, aiming to preserve their own unique populations of horses that are only present in small numbers. In the US, for instance, the American Livestock Breeds Conservancy lists as 'Critical' breeds that consist of fewer than 2,000 individuals around the world and 200 registrations in the US each year. On this list are the Caspian, Cleveland Bay, Exmoor Pony and Suffolk, as well as the Florida Cracker, descended from Iberian breeds taken to North America in the 16th century, and the American Cream Draught, derived from a single mare first put up for sale in 1911.

The list of the Rare Breeds Trust of Australia, as well as the Caspian, Suffolk and Cleveland Bay carries more unusual breeds such as the Timor Pony, a jack-of-all-trades probably originally developed from horses taken to the Indonesian island of Timor from India. The Australian list also includes a unique Aussie breed, the Waler. This breed was developed from English horses sent out to the Australian colony in the 18th century, including Clydesdales and Thoroughbreds, as well as horses from the Cape of Good Hope, and Timor ponies. The name was originally 'New South Waler', which identified the horse in India during the British Raj, when the breed was imported for polo and riding, as well as for cavalry use. The Waler became legendary for its courage and endurance during the First World War.

Other rare breeds have been saved from extinction by breed societies around the world, though many are still under threat. In Russia, for example, the Orlov-Rostopchin and the Orlov Trotter are endangered. The Trotter was developed in the late 1700s by Count Alexei Orlov-Chesmensky from Thoroughbreds and a host of Danish, Russian and Spanish breeds, as well as Persian 'Arabians' (probably the Akhal-Teke). He also developed the Orlov Riding Horse from his foundation mares in response to the demand for dressage horses from the upper classes. Around the same time, a rival breeder, Count Fyodor Vasilyevich Rostopchin, produced a black saddle horse from Arabians and Thoroughbreds, which was slightly smaller and faster. In 1845, when both breeders had died, the state bought both studs and began combining the Olov Riding Horse and the Rostopchin Riding Horse into the Orlov-Rostopchin, now known as the Russian Riding Horse. Most of the horses died during the two world wars and in a stud farm fire, but attempts were made to rejuvenate the breed in the 1930s and 1950s. Interest has been sparked by imports into the US, but breed numbers are still small.

In Slovenia, a studbook for the Posavje was started in 1993. The Posavje is a cold-blooded horse originating in the remote wetlands of northwest Croatia, its isolation protecting it from being crossed with the Ardennes and Belgians used for agriculture in the rest of the region. The Posavje was recorded more than 100 years ago, and was used to pull trams in Vienna and Budapest. The population declined in the 20th century, and the studbook was begun with only 109 mares and 10 stallions.

Other critically endangered native breeds include the Arenberg-Nordkirchen and Rottal in Germany, the Monterufoli Pony and Rapid Heavy Draught in Italy, and the Zemaituka from Lithuania – but these are just a few of many.

So what's the prospect for endangered breeds?

"The RBST has several ongoing projects which are targeted at equines," says Dawn Teverson. "Firstly, by listing the rare equine breeds, they are eligible for a substantial grant from the Horserace Betting Levy Board. In many cases, the breed societies would by unsustainable without this grant. The Trust is collecting and studying equine DNA in order to produce breed profiles of our listed rare native breeds, and is also collecting semen from stallions, which will be archived as well as being used for conservation breeding. Genetic bloodline analyses have been conducted on several equine breeds, using specially developed software. We have identified rare bloodlines and use the information generated to maximise the genetic health of the breed by informing both in situ and ex situ conservation programmes.

"The prospects of the breeds on the RBST Watchlist are good, as long as we can continue to work together with breed societies to support them and implement proposed conservation measures."

What about cloning? If techniques are improved so that more embryos survive, could endangered breeds be saved as exact copies of the last few individuals? Prof. Gordon Woods, who cloned the first mules, thinks this is certainly possible. "This has already been done with endangered or exotic cattle and sheep [such as Enderby Island cattle, cloned from the last cow], so I see no reason why it can't be successfully done with endangered equine species or breeds."

However, bringing back extinct breeds by cloning is a different matter, he adds. "Currently, cloning technology requires living or viable cellular material from the animal to be cloned, which will probably preclude the ability to clone an extinct animal at this time (it was recently attempted with the extinct Tasmanian Tiger in Australia). Besides the technical challenges, it will require a large financial commitment to use cloning for the preservation of endangered species."

In the end, the best course of action seems to be to not let the breed become extinct in the first place. After all, humans have had a hand in the horse's life for millennia, so it is our responsibility. As Dawn Teverson points out, "even the 'wild' Exmoor ponies living on Exmoor are carefully managed and stallions are changed on the decision of the owner. All extra colts are gelded, so even here breeding is highly managed by man."

While humans have been responsible for the extinction of many breeds – either through artificial selection; changing them to something else; change of use (as in allowing heavy horses to decline after mechanization); or from simple neglect – we also have the power to preserve them.

From the searing heat of the desert to icy northern wastes; windswept rocky islands to the dry, dusty steppe; horses have adapted to life across the globe, whether in the company of people or fending for themselves. And while this is a affirmation of the horse's success as a species, it also highlights how the horse has contributed to our own success: some would say being responsible for the spread of humankind across the world. If those people in long-ago Ukraine had not first attempted to ride or herd wild horses, would there have been the widespread migrations, wars and resettlements of history, and the sharing of culture and the arts between disparate populations? Would there have been the wheel, the haulage harness, mechanised agriculture – even trousers?

While it's likely that all the things we now take for granted would have eventually been invented or discovered even without the horse, there's no doubt that *Equus caballus* probably speeded up many changes and played a major part in the development of human civilisation. So now that we have the know-how and ability to alter the very environment in which we and other species live, perhaps it's time we gave something back.

Morgan
© *Lynn Parr*

Further Information

Caspian

The Caspian Horse Society (UK)
www.caspianhorsesociety.org.uk

The International Caspian Society
www.caspianhorses.org

The Caspian Horse Society of the Americas
www.caspian.org

The Australasian Caspian Society
http://australasiancaspiansociety.org

Friesian

Friesians Scotland
www.friesiansscotland.com

The Friesian Horse Association of Great Britain and Ireland
www.fhagbi.co.uk

The Friesian Horse Society
www.friesianhorsesociety.com

Kerry Bog

The Kerry Bog Pony Society
www.kerrybogpony.ie

The American Kerry Bog Pony Society
www.kerrybogpony.org/

Eriskay

The Eriskay Pony (Purebred) Studbook Society
www.eriskaypony.org.uk

The Eriskay Pony Society
www.eriskaypony.com

Marwari
>The Indigenous Horse Society of India
>*www.horsemarwari.com*
>*http://horseindian.com/index.htm*

>Friends of Marwari/Kathiawari Horse UK
>*http://friendsofmarwari.org.uk*

Takhi
>International Takhi Group
>*www.savethewildhorse.org*

>Association Pour le Cheval de Przewalski
>*www.takh.org*

Carneddau
>Merlod y Carneddau
>*www.carneddauponies.co.uk*

Sorraia
>Sorraia Information Site
>*www.sorraia.org*

>Sorraia Mustang Info Page
>*www.spanish-mustang.org/*

Mustang
>National Wild Horse and Burro Program
>*www.blm.gov/wo/st/en/prog/whbprogram.html*

>International Society for the Protection of Mustangs & Burros
>*www.ispmb.org/*

>The Spanish Mustang Registry Inc.
>*www.spanishmustang.org/*

Spanish Mustangs UK
www.spanishmustangs.org.uk/index.php/

Saving America's Mustangs Foundation
www.savingamericasmustangs.org

Konik Polski
The Wicken Fen Vision
www.equiculture.com.au/CLM91wickenfen.pdf

Cloning
BBC News: First Cloned Horse Unveiled in Italy
http://news.bbc.co.uk/1/hi/sci/tech/3129441.stm

National Geographic News
http://news.nationalgeographic.com/news/2006/04/0404_060404_horse_clone.html

Horse Genetics
The Horse Genome Project
www.uky.edu/Ag/Horsemap/welcome.html

The Rare Breed Survival Trust
https://www.rbst.org.uk

The American Livestock Breeds Conservancy
www.albc-usa.org

The Rare Breeds Trust of Australia
rarebreedstrust.com.au

Acknowledgements

Many thanks to all the breeders, breed societies and experts who contributed photographs and checked and amended the text. If you spot something that needs updating, please get in touch with the author at info@lynnparr.co.uk and it will be corrected with the next edition.

The digital version of this text can be found at www.amazon.co.uk and www.amazon.com.

Author's Note

This book only covers a few breeds and the stories of a few people. There are numerous other breeds around the world either in danger or rescued, as well as many, many more people deserving of praise for their tireless efforts on behalf of the horse. Likewise, this book only represents the views of a handful of people (not necessarily the author), and other people may have contrary views on the best way to save certain breeds, methods of study and management, historical interpretation, or even what a breed should be called. Scientific information changes all the time and people change their minds.

For now, however, let's put aside all our differences and just celebrate that wonderful animal we have come to know as our friend: the Horse.

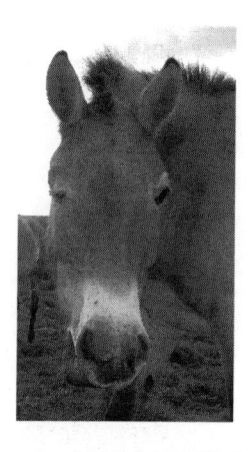

(courtesy of Suffolk Wildlife Trust)